The Early Release Provision

How to Reduce Your Sentence by 95%

Written by:
David Mathis

CP

Cadmus Publishing
www.cadmuspublishing.com

Published by Cadmus Publishing
www.cadmuspublishing.com
Port Angeles, WA

ISBN: 978-1-63751-098-8

For Brenda Sue

Vigilantibus et non dormientibus jura subveniunt
(The laws aid the vigilant, not those who sleep)

Table of Contents

INTRODUCTION

―――――――∞◦〰◦∞―――――――

You have been indicted for violating federal or state law, convicted of the charge, and sentenced by the judge. What should you do now? If you are like me, your thoughts have immediately turned to getting out of prison as soon as possible. What I did about my situation, however, was try to escape by building a hang glider. That turned my situation from bad to worse. I was given a new charge, convicted, and had years added to my already lengthy federal sentence. Further, I lost two months of good-time credit. I was placed in the Bureau of Prisons' (BOP) two-hour watch program, and I was sent to a federal penitentiary (maximum security) for ten years. Within hours of my arrival at the penitentiary, two guys were murdered. We spent months on lockdown. You do not want to follow my example. Trust me on this!

I was a first-time offender when I first entered federal prison many years ago. I did not know the law or the fact that there were a number of ways that I could legally reduce my sentence. Back then, before the Supreme Court of the United States decided the case of *United States v. Booker*, 543 U.S. 220 (2005), we were told that the United States Sentencing Guidelines were mandatory and that the only way to reduce a federal sentence was to cooperate with the Government. A great many federal defendants did not cooperate. But because we did not know that early release opportunities existed, we simply did our time. Mostly, this was due to the fact that there were no lawyers or prisoners advising us about possible early release programs. Nor were there any books that one could read and learn how to apply for early release. Therefore, I followed the route that many "jailhouse lawyers" pursued. I began studying federal law in the prison's law library. Then I attacked my conviction and sentence in federal court. I filed a motion to vacate my conviction and sentence pursuant to Title 28, United States Code, section 2255. The results were predictable given my lack of legal knowledge and the one-year time limit I had to file my claims. My §2255 motion was denied.

After that denial, I made the conscious decision that if I could not get relief for myself, I would at least help as many other prisoners as possible get the relief that they deserved. That became my motivation.

Through the years, my education and legal knowledge grew. I earned a Bachelor of Arts degree from West Virginia University. Later, I earned a Paralegal diploma from Blackstone Career Institute and a Paralegal certificate from Adams State University. In addition, I succeeded in overturning an array of convictions and reducing the sentences of many prisoners.

But as the years wore on, I began to notice two disturbing facts. First, I noticed that more and more of the new people who were entering federal prison had never dealt with the federal criminal justice system. A person would come into the system without a clue as to how he or she should proceed with his or her case. In this regard, these new prisoners were experiencing the same problem that I faced when I first came into the system in 1994. As a result, the period for filing a §2255 motion had usually expired by the time the person came to me for help. I cannot count the number of times that someone has approached me seeking assistance and I would find that the person had valid claims, but that the person had allowed his one-year limitation period to elapse. Usually, any §2255 motion that I filed on such a person's behalf was denied by the district court as untimely. The second fact that I noticed was that the trial courts were granting less and less relief. It became almost impossible to overturn a conviction in the federal courts. Even when the facts and law supported the prisoner's case, the court would routinely take years to decide the issue and most often, only after the person had already completed his or her sentence.

These combined factors eventually caused me to start searching for other ways to reduce a person's prison sentence. Through my research, I was able to uncover a number of early release opportunities that were available to federal and state prisoners. I then began helping prisoners implement these early release strategies. For example, I met a prisoner named Troy while we were at the federal penitentiary in Jonesville, Virginia. Troy had been given a 10-year mandatory minimum term of imprisonment, to be followed by 5 years of supervised release, as the result of a drug conspiracy conviction. This was his first federal sentence, though he had previously done time in county jails. Troy was basically in shock when I first met him because he never believed

3

that he would get so much time, especially given the fact that the police had not recovered any drugs in his possession.

At his first unit team review, his case manager gave him a copy of his sentence computation form. This form showed that he was eligible for about 500 days of good-time credit. Using this form and a Good Time Table, I was able to explain to Troy that if he kept out of trouble and participated in various programming activities, he would essentially reduce his sentence to 8 years, 8 months. I also explained to him that he was eligible for up to one-year off his sentence if he completed the Residential Drug Abuse Program, known as RDAP. That information lit a spark in him.

Over the next three years, Troy took every class that was offered at the prison, completed the 40-hour drug treatment program (non-RDAP), and worked at the prison's UNICOR factory. When his security points dropped, he was transferred to a medium security prison which had the 500- hour residential drug program. Fortunately, we were able to keep in contact with each other with the assistance of his sister. Troy completed RDAP and earned one year off his sentence. Troy's situation became even more interesting with the passage of the Second Chance Act in 2008. That law gave Troy and other prisoners an opportunity to be eligible for up to one-year of halfway house placement. (With the passage of the First Step Act in 2018, some federal prisoners now earn years of halfway house placement or home confinement). When Troy was 19 months from his release date, I wrote him a Second Chance Act memorandum for him to present to his unit team. He subsequently received 11 months of halfway house placement. Thus, Troy served a total of 6 years, 9 months behind prison walls. Stated another way, Troy served only 67.5% of his time in federal prison—when the average federal prisoner was serving 85% of his or her time in federal prison. I was later able to reduce Troy's term of supervised release by nearly 80%.

After years of successfully helping prisoners like Troy reduce their sentences, I decided to write a series of books to make the information available to anyone who is entering or has entered the federal or state criminal justice system. It is my fervent hope to make as many people as possible aware of the opportunities that they may not have known about or even considered. Indeed, if I had known about these opportunities when I first entered the system, my federal time would have been a whole lot different—and shorter.

Each book in the series is packed full of proven methods that have allowed federal and state prisoners to successfully reduce their sentences. Each book also gives easy to follow, step-by-step instructions on how to fill out petitions or letters and send them to the appropriate federal or state agency. Moreover, each book contains real life, easy-to-understand examples that you can use as templates for developing your own petitions or letters. Best of all, these books allow you to seek early release without having to spend hours upon hours in the law library or pay for the services of an attorney or jailhouse lawyer.

The Early Release Provision is the second book in the series.[1] It describes federal and state laws which give federal and state "non-U.S. citizen" prisoners an opportunity to reduce their sentences (in some cases by more than 95%), leave prison, and return home.

These laws have been on the books for many years. Yet, for a host of reasons, most federal and state prisoners (as well as prison staff) are unaware of their existence. And of those prisoners who are aware of these laws, many do not know how to apply for these types of early release programs.

---

[1] The first book is *Pardons and Commutations of Sentences: The Complete Guidebook to Applying for Clemency*. It is published by Prisology Press.

The Early Release Provision, however, solves these problems (and many more) for you by providing you with the steps that you will need to follow in order to obtain your early release.

Please read on if you are interested in reducing your sentence and earning your valuable freedom.

CHAPTER 1
HELPFUL TIPS

—◇o〰o◇—

Before we discuss the opportunities listed in this book, the following chapter is designed to provide you with some helpful tips so that you can maximize your chances of success. These tips are important, regardless of whether you have just been arrested, nearing the end of your sentence, or somewhere in between.

Tip No. 1 — MAINTAIN A "CLEAR" PRISON CONDUCT RECORD

One of the ways that prison staff, parole officers, judges, and others determine whether an individual has modified his or her behavior is based upon the person's prison conduct record. The thinking goes like this: If a person is unable to maintain clear conduct while he or she is incarcerated, what chance does that same person have of living within the law if he or she is released?

A typical example of this type of thinking can be found in the following true-life situation: A California prisoner was eligible for parole after serving more than 17 years in state prison. Prior to his appearance before the parole board, the prisoner had high hopes that he would be granted parole. This hope was based on the amount of time that he had spent in prison and the classes that he had recently completed. The parole board granted him a tentative parole release date. However, the board's decision was reversed by the governor, who found that "given the current record before me and after carefully considering the same factors the Board must consider, I believe [the prisoner's] release from prison would pose an unreasonable risk of danger to society at this time." What was the primary factor that caused the governor to deny parole to this prisoner? It was the prisoner's prison conduct record, which included infractions for making threats against a correctional officer, refusing a direct order, and gambling.

I believe that good prison conduct is the most important factor when it comes to any type of early release. Even if the requested early release does not center around prison conduct—for example, you are seeking compassionate release—your prison conduct (especially if it is negative) will still be given great weight when a decision is made.

Under federal and most state laws, a prisoner receives varying amounts of "good-time" credit towards a reduction in the amount of time that he or she must serve in prison simply by obeying prison rules. Of course, the opposite is true as well. When a prisoner violates the rules of the prison, good time credit may be withheld or even taken, thereby extending the amount of time that the prisoner must serve behind bars. Thus, it is very important that you heed this first tip and maintain a clear prison conduct record.

Tip No. 2 — TAKE FULL ADVANTAGE OF ANY AVAILABLE EDUCATIONAL OPPORTUNITIES

By participating in educational pursuits, you will not only improve your chances of success, but you will use your prison time in a productive manner, give yourself more career paths to choose from, and become more knowledgeable about the world around you.

There are numerous types and levels of educational programs offered at each federal and state prison. The programs may include General Equivalency Development (GED) classes, for example. It is worth noting here that obtaining your GED, if you do not have one, has significant financial benefits. Statistics have shown that a person with a high school diploma or GED makes almost $10,000 more per year than someone who does not have a high school diploma or GED. Other programs offered may include Adult Continuing Education (ACE) classes, such as public speaking, business ownership, parenting, and job interviewing skills; as well as Vocational Trade (VT) classes like masonry, building maintenance, office machine repair, and welding. A few prisons also offer apprenticeship programs and college courses. For instance, a federal prison (Herlong, California) and a state prison (Susanville, California), about an hour away from each other, offer California prisoners an opportunity to take college classes through Lassen Community College. These prisoners can earn an associate degree, free of charge.

Moreover, at most federal and state prisons, the Psychology Department offers anger management, residential or non-residential drug and alcohol treatment, alternatives-to-violence, and various self-help classes.

As an added bonus, in many states, and now the federal prison system participation in the above type of classes can earn a prisoner "earned time" credit. This credit helps the prisoner reduce his or her prison time, similar to good time credit or allow them additional halfway house and/or home confinement placement.

The thing to remember is that federal and state laws are constantly changing. When you first enter the criminal justice system, it may seem likely that you will have to complete your entire prison sentence or most of it. This may cause you to abandon any educational pursuits or recklessly accumulate disciplinary reports. Nevertheless, in all likelihood, a new law, regulation, or policy will be passed that will allow you to reduce your prison time. By way of example, since 2007, the United States Sentencing Commission has lowered the sentencing levels for crack cocaine offenses three times, allowing thousands of federal prisoners to go home early.

Tip No.3 — AVOID GAMBLING, DRUG/ALCOHOL, AND OTHER NEGATIVE INFLUENCES

More deaths and acts of violence occur in federal and state prisons because of gambling debts and drug and alcohol abuse than any other factors. The situation has become so bad that the Bureau of Prisons (BOP) has tried a number of ways to combat the problem. The BOP's actions have included removing fruit juices and sugar from most of its prison commissaries (stores) and dining halls, limiting the amount of stamps a prisoner can purchase, and increasing the penalties for prisoners found gambling or intoxicated. Many state departments of corrections (DOC) have taken similar precautions.

Of course, many people find ways around such restrictions and will try to entice you into following their lead. Do not be tempted. When you drink or do drugs, you lose mental control and possible physical control of your body. You will do things that you would not normally do or you will make yourself vulnerable to others. The following is a tragic example.

When I was at a maximum security prison in Virginia, I met a person named Ernest. Ernest was in his mid-30s and had a 30-year sentence. When I first met him, Ernest was just starting to take classes and do other types of programs in an effort to be transferred to a medium security prison. During our time together at that facility, we had often seen or heard about intoxicated people being raped, beaten, or stabbed. On several occasions, we had talked about the dangers of drinking or taking drugs, especially in a prison setting. I believed that Ernest was on the right track. I left the prison five years after I had arrived. Ernest was still at the prison when I left. I was on my way to a medium security prison in California when I heard the news that Ernest had been killed. According to one witness, Ernest had been drunk when he was killed. Prior to his death, he had been at a gambling table and had begun to verbally disrespect another prisoner at the table. When Ernest went back to his cell, the other prisoner followed him to the cell and stabbed him to death.

Likewise, gambling debts can cause you to lose either financial or emotional control. You may lose hundreds or thousands of dollars at the gambling table. You will find yourself in a situation where you have to give your hard earned money to someone else. On the other hand, perhaps, you were "lucky" and won a few hundred dollars, at least on paper. However, what will you do if the other gamblers cannot pay their debts? This happens more often than not. You will have either to swallow the debt or collect it through violence. At the moment when you find out that you will not be paid, you probably will not be thinking about the serious repercussions that may arise for all concerned parties. You will just want your money.

A few years ago, a guy ran into that exact situation. It happened at a state prison in Pennsylvania. The guy was owed $50 in gambling debt by another prisoner. When the guy was not paid in a timely fashion, he beat the other guy so severely that the other guy lost part of his memory. As a result of this one event, both guys paid a heavy price. One guy permanently lost part of his memory while the other guy was convicted of aggravated assault and given more prison time. Remember, all of this occurred over a $50 gambling debt.

Is substance abuse or gambling really the route that you want to take if you are serious about getting out of prison early so that you can be with your loved ones?

Tip No. 4 — REMAIN EMPLOYED THROUGHOUT YOUR PRISON SENTENCE

Employment is one of the most effective rehabilitative tools you can have in your toolbox. First, of course, it provides you with money to pay for your various wants and needs. Second, it can provide you with hands-on work experience. Third, your prison supervisor could potentially serve as a job reference for you upon your release from prison.

Ideally, the employment that you seek should involve developing "transferable skills." These are skills that can be used in prison but more importantly, they can be used after you are released. One of the best ways of obtaining this type of skill is by enrolling in an apprenticeship program. Participants in these types of programs obtain book knowledge as well as hands-on experience. In addition, upon completion of an apprenticeship program, the person usually gets a certificate from the U.S. Department of Labor, which certifies that the person has completed the requisite number of hours of labor and coursework.

If there is no apprenticeship program offered at your facility, you may be able to get the same effect by combining VT training with a similar type of employment. If, for instance, the prison offers VT plumbing, you could complete the vocational trade training and then work in the plumbing shop in the Facilities or Maintenance Department. However, since you will not get an apprenticeship certificate from the U.S. Department of Labor, you should keep a copy of your VT certificate (plus a copy of the VT class curriculum, if any) and copies of your payroll sheets, which are generally kept in your inmate file or the files of the department in which you worked. Legally, under federal and various state employment laws, prisons are required to maintain prisoners' payroll records for a number of years—even if the prisoner has been released—due to potential worker's compensation or other employment related claims. You can show this material to any potential employer as evidence of your completed coursework and work experience. The possibilities are endless. You just have to use a little imagination, make a plan, and follow through with it.

With regards to early release, if you are a state prisoner, you may be able to get "earned time" credit for your work participation. This can reduce the amount of time that you spend in prison. In fact, in a number of states, a prisoner may be given earned time credit rather than a paycheck for his or her work. While in other states, a prisoner may get both a paycheck and earned time credit. As stated earlier BOP inmates can use their earned time credit for extended halfway house or home confinement placement.

Tip No. 5 — GARNER SUPPORT FROM FAMILY, FRIENDS, AND COMMUNITY MEMBERS

The more people who rally to support you, the better chances you have at succeeding in life, in general, and reducing your prison time, in particular. When the time comes for you to apply for early release or a reduced sentence, you should have family members, friends, and community members (such as a former employer) write letters on your behalf attesting to the positive things that you did before you were arrested and the positive things that you have done since you have been incarcerated.

One thing that you will learn quickly, if you have not already done so, is that "friends" begin to fall off the moment that you are arrested. They disappear even faster once you are sent to prison. You are no longer an integral part of their lives. As the saying goes, "out of sight, out of mind." It is your responsibility, however, to remain constantly on their minds. You do not have to call, write, or e-mail them everyday to accomplish this task. Rather, it may be more feasible (and cheaper) for you to contact them on a weekly or monthly basis. You should use all available communication modes, i.e., letters, e-mails, telephone calls, and visits, to remain in contact with people. A few words of caution, however. While communicating with people, you should refrain from constantly asking them for money. People will begin to feel that you are contacting them simply to get money. They will eventually stop writing to you or accepting your calls or e-mails.

Remember, it is always best to build bridges rather than burn them down. This is especially true in those states in which the DOC requires a prisoner to have a valid release plan before the DOC will release that prisoner. Any release plan may require that the prisoner have a place to stay and a possible job lined up. These requirements are more easily met if you have maintained contact with your family, friends, and former employer.

The aforementioned general tips apply to every state and federal prisoner, especially if he or she is just coming into the criminal justice system.

In addition, throughout this book there may be terms that are unfamiliar to you. For that reason, the following is a glossary of the terms that will appear throughout this book:

Aggravated Felony: A felony made worse or more serious by circumstances such as violence, the presence of a deadly weapon, intent to commit another crime, or intent to cause harm or reckless disregard for another's safety.

Alien/Migrant: A foreign-born person in the United States who has not become a U.S. citizen and is still a citizen of another country. Can refer to legal immigrants as well as "illegal" immigrants.

Amnesty: A general pardon that is granted to a group or class of people rather than an individual.

Attorney General: The chief law officer of the United States or a state who is responsible for advising the government on legal matters and who represents the government in litigation.

Board of Pardons: The Board of Pardons, which generally consists of the governor, secretary of state, and attorney general, may have the authority to remit fines, forfeitures, and/or restitution; grant reprieves and pardons; and commute sentences in criminal cases, except case of impeachment and sometimes cases of treason.

Clemency: Mercy or leniency granted to a person in the form of a pardon, reprieve, commutation of sentence, and/or remittance of fine or restitution. Generally termed executive clemency when it is granted by the head of the executive branch of a government such as the president for the federal government and a governor for a state government.

Commutation of Sentence: A commutation of sentence is a reduction or lessening of the original sentence or penalty. Generally, it takes the form of a reduction in the length of imprisonment. In some cases, it may result in immediate release from prison.

Criminal Alien: Commonly referred to as an "illegal alien," it is a foreign-born person who lacks a right to be in the United States; normally one who has entered the U.S. without inspection or permission or has illegally returned after being deported or removed.

Department of Corrections (DOC): A principal branch or division of a state government that oversees that state's penal and correction facilities.

Immigration and Customs Enforcement (ICE): An investigative branch of the Department of Homeland Security responsible for enforcing federal laws pertaining to border control, customs, and immigration.

Immigration and Naturalization Service (INS): The former U.S. Department of Justice agency that administered the INS Act and operated the U.S. Border Patrol. The INS ceased to exist on March 1, 2003.

Memorandum of Agreement (MOA): A written statement or letter of intent that details an agreement or understanding of parties who plan to enter into a contract or other type of agreement. Also known as a Memorandum of Understanding (MOU).

Pardon Attorney: An attorney with the U.S. Department of Justice who receives and reviews all federal executive clemency petitions, initiates the necessary investigations, and prepares a report and recommendation for submission to the President of the United States.

Parole: The conditional release of a prisoner from imprisonment before the full sentence has been served. It is usually granted for good behavior on the condition that the person regularly report to a supervising or parole officer for a specified period.

Parole Board: A government body that decides whether prisoners may be released from prison before completing their sentence. In some states, it is known as a Board of Paroles and Pardons.

Supervised Release: A period of probation that is imposed in addition to a sentence of imprisonment rather than as a substitute for part or all of a sentence. A violation of the terms of supervised release may result in imprisonment. Also known as parole supervision in some states.

Suspended Sentence: A criminal sentence that is not enforced unless the defendant violates any conditions or terms set by the court (such as committing a new crime).

CHAPTER 2
IMMIGRATION AND CUSTOMS ENFORCEMENT (ICE) POLICIES AND PRACTICES

———◇o◠◡◠o◇———

The United States Immigration and Customs Enforcement (ICE) is an agency within the Department of Homeland Security. According to its Criminal Alien Program Handbook, one of its most important mandates "is the enhancement of public safety and the security of the American public." Under its broad authority, ICE identifies and removes "dangerous, often recidivist, criminal aliens engaged in crimes such as murder, predatory sexual offenses, narcotics trafficking, alien smuggling, and a host of other crimes that have a profoundly negative impact on our society."

In order to support its mandate, ICE developed—through its Criminal Alien Division (CAD)—the Criminal Alien Program (CAP). CAP's mission is to provide agency-wide support in the identification and apprehension of criminal aliens who are incarcerated within federal and state prisons and local jails. ICE officials attempt to process these aliens expeditiously in order to secure a final order of removal for them before they are released to ICE custody. "The identification and processing of incarcerated criminal aliens, before release from jails and prisons, decreases or eliminates the time spent in ICE custody awaiting removal, thereby reducing the overall cost to the federal government." Additionally, CAP officials, in conjunction with the various U.S. Attorney's offices across the country, assist in the preparation and criminal prosecution of those who violate criminal immigration laws.

CAP oversees a number of initiatives designed to help it accomplish its mission, including the Violent Criminal Alien Section (VCAS), the Joint Criminal Alien Removal Taskforce (JCART), and the Law Enforcement Agency Response Unit (LEAR). As will be discussed in a later chapter, CAP also oversees the Rapid Repatriation of Eligible Parolees Accepted for Transfer (Rapid REPAT), a joint partnership with state correctional/parole agencies designed to expedite the process of allowing selected non-violent criminal aliens incarcerated in U.S. prisons and jails to accept early release in exchange for voluntarily returning to their country of origin. See Figure 2-1.

Criminal Alien Program (CAP) Initiatives

- **Violent Criminal Alien Section (VCAS)**
  The primary responsibility of VCAS is to enforce violations of criminal immigration law, mainly through the activities of Enforcement and Removal Operations (ERO).

- **Joint Criminal Alien Removal Taskforce (JCART)**
  JCART is responsible for the identification, investigation, and arrest of at-large criminal aliens with convictions for crimes such as drug trafficking, crimes of violence, and sex offenses. JCART partners with other agencies such as the United States Marshals Service, U.S. Customs and Border Protection, and local law enforcement departments.

- **Law Enforcement Agency Response Unit (LEAR)**
  LEAR provides 24/7 response to all calls for assistance from state and local law enforcement agencies related to suspected immigration law violators.

- **U.S. Citizenship and Immigration Services (USCIS) Referrals**
  ERO officers receive and investigate referrals from USCIS in order to place into removal proceedings those applicants who have been denied immigration benefits.

- **Rapid Repatriation of Eligible Parolees Accepted for Transfer (Rapid REPAT)**
  Rapid REPAT is a joint partnership with state correctional/parole agencies designed to expedite the process of allowing select non-violent criminal aliens incarcerated in U.S. prisons and jails to accept early release in exchange for voluntarily returning to their country of origin.

Figure 2-1

The remainder of this chapter provides you with some of the policies and practices that are followed by ICE personnel performing CAP duties. This section is intended to provide you with a broad understanding of how ICE personnel identify criminal aliens in federal, state, and local correctional facilities, prepare and send detainers, and initiate removal proceedings and obtain final orders of removal and warrants.

By understanding these policies and practices, you will better to be able to ascertain the priorities of ICE personnel, determine your place within that hierarchy, and select the best available option for your specific situation.

For example, let us say that a person has just been arrested by local law enforcement officials for possession of a firearm by a felon. When his arrest is entered into the law enforcement database, an alert ICE agent discovers that the person has entered the country illegally and that a prior order of removal had been issued. The ICE agent immediately sends a detainer request (I-247 form) to the local law enforcement agency, asking that the arrestee be detained until ICE can take custody of that person. Because of his prior deportation and state conviction, the person knows that there is a high probability that his removal order will be reinstated. More concerning to the person, however, is the fact that he could be prosecuted in federal court for illegal re-entry and firearm possession. He would face up to 20 years in federal prison if he is convicted. Knowing the possible consequences of his situation, and the fact that ICE personnel like to obtain a final removal order before sending the case to the U.S. Attorney's office for prosecution, the person asks his defense attorney to immediately negotiate a plea agreement with the local District Attorney's office.

Due to the defendant's awareness of ICE's policies and practices, he was able to obtain a favorable plea agreement in which he received a suspended sentence and spent only 148 days in county jail (about 4% of his possible state sentence) before he was placed in ICE's custody and quickly deported. Most importantly, he did not get prosecuted in federal court and thus, he avoided a 20-year federal prison sentence. The above scenario is based on a real-life Mississippi case; a story that you will read about in Chapter 5.

Please take a moment to think about what this person was able to accomplish—all because he was aware of ICE's policies and practices. He actually received a 10-year sentence in state court, but the judge suspended 9 years and 364 days of that sentence (meaning the person served one day on his sentence). He also spent 148 days in the county jail while the plea was being negotiated. This amounted to this person serving only 4% of his potential state sentence. Finally, he completely avoided federal prosecution and a 20-year federal sentence. It was a win-win-win situation for the state, ICE, and of course, the defendant. The state obtained a conviction. It also avoided a trial, appeal, and incarceration costs. ICE avoided a lengthy removal process and detention cost. It also quickly removed a dangerous, and potentially violent person from the United States. The benefits to the defendant were immeasurable.

The following is how immigration cases **generally** proceed:

1. **Criminal Arrest**

When a person is arrested by a local, state or federal law enforcement officer (LEO), the LEO obtains the arrestee's biographical data, such as name; date of birth; and social security number. The LEO also obtains the arrestee's biometric information, normally a set of fingerprints. With this information, the LEO searches various databases such as the NCIC for the arrestee's prior criminal records. More recently LEOs have been able to utilize federal information-sharing databases. These databases include the Department of Homeland Security's Automated Biometric Identification System (IDENT) and the Department of Justice's Integrated Automated Fingerprint Identification System (IAFIS).

Behind the scene, immigration officials, generally ERO officers, utilize various databases like IDENT and IAFIS to conduct daily reviews of local, state, and federal arrests, to determine if any of the arrestees are in the country illegally.

2. **Immigration Detainer**

Once a preliminary review indicates that an arrestee may be in the country illegally, immigration officials issue an immigration detainer (I-247 form) to local, state, and federal law enforcement agencies, providing those agencies with notice of ICE's intent to assume custody of an arrestee.

Immigration detainers have three key functions: (1) to notify a law enforcement agency that ICE intends to arrest or remove an alien in the law enforcement agency's custody once the alien is no longer subject to that agency's detention; (2) to request information from a law enforcement agency about an alien's impending release so that ICE may assume custody before the alien is released; and (3) to request that the law enforcement agency maintain custody of an alien who would otherwise be released for a period not to exceed 48 hours (excluding Saturdays, Sundays, and holidays) to provide ICE time to assume custody.

It is important to note that immigration officials issue detainers to a law enforcement agency only after the law enforcement agency exercised its independent authority to arrest a person for a criminal violation. Moreover, immigration officials are given discretion over whether to issue an immigration detainer, even if it has been conclusively determined that the person is in the country illegally.

An example of this occurred when a person was arrested by officers with the Pittsburgh Police Department and transported to the Allegheny County Jail. After jail officials obtained the person's biographical and biometric data, they entered it into their law enforcement computer system, where an ICE agent noticed that the person was in the country illegally. The agent now needs to make a decision on whether to issue an immigration detainer. Because the person has lived in the country for the past ten years, has no past crimes of violence or aggravated felonies, and has been charged with public intoxication—a summary offense in Pennsylvania—the ICE agent does not issue an immigration detainer. Simply put, the ICE agent had higher priorities, which you will learn about shortly.

One of the better things about the Allegheny County Jail is the fact that an inmate can go to the pod (unit) officer and have the officer look up the inmate's status on the jail's computer. The person may have a charge but could be released because the judge granted him or her bail. However, when the person looks at the computer screen that line item is red. That is because the person's family has not posted the bail yet. Once they do, the line item on the screen will turn to green. Similarly, if the ICE agent had issued an immigration detainer, the immigration line item on the screen would have appeared in red. I mention this information here because these types of tools can help you quickly determine whether you are on ICE's radar screen.

3. **Priorities for the Apprehension, Detention, and Removal of Aliens**

In light of the large number of immigration law violations that ICE is charged with addressing and its limited resources, the agency must prioritize the use of its enforcement personnel, detention space, and removal resources.

The following constitutes ICE's enforcement priorities, with the first being the highest priority and the second and third constituting equal, but lower priorities.

Priority 1: Aliens who pose a danger to national security or a risk to public security. These aliens include, but are not limited to:

- Aliens engaged in or suspected of terrorism or espionage, or who otherwise pose a danger to national security;
- Aliens convicted of crimes, with a particular emphasis on violent criminals, felons, and repeat offenders;
- Aliens not younger than 16 years of age who participated in organized criminal gangs;
- Aliens subject to outstanding criminal warrants; and
- Aliens who otherwise pose a serious risk to public safety.

For purposes of prioritizing the removal of aliens convicted of crimes, ICE personnel use the following offense levels, with Level 1 and Level 2 offenders receiving principal attention.

- Level 1 offenders: aliens convicted of "aggravated felonies," as defined in INA § 101(a)(43) of the Immigration and Nationality Act, or two or more crimes, each punishable by more than one year, commonly referred to as "felonies";
- Level 2 offenders: aliens convicted of any felony or three or more crimes, each punishable by less than one year, commonly referred to as "misdemeanors"; and
- Level 3 offenders: aliens convicted of crimes punishable by less than one year.

Priority 2: Recent illegal entrants.

Next, in order to maintain control at the border and at ports of entry, and to avoid a return to the prior practice commonly and historically referred to as "catch and release," the removal of aliens who have recently violated immigration controls at the border, at ports of entry, or through the knowing abuse of the visa and visa waiver programs are next on ICE's priority list.

Priority 3: Aliens who are fugitives or otherwise obstruct immigration controls.

The removal of aliens who are subject to a final order of removal and who abscond, fail to depart, or intentionally obstruct immigration controls are last on ICE's priority list. These aliens include:

- Fugitive aliens, in descending priority as follows:
- o fugitive aliens who pose a danger to national security;
- o fugitive aliens convicted of violent crimes or who otherwise pose a threat to the community;
- o fugitive aliens with criminal convictions other than a violent crime;
- o fugitive aliens who have not been convicted of a crime.
- Aliens who reenter the country illegally after removal, in descending priority as follows:
- o previously removed aliens who pose a danger to national security;
- o previously removed aliens convicted of violent crimes or who otherwise pose a threat to the community;
- o previously removed aliens with criminal convictions other than a violent crime;
- o previously removed aliens who have not been convicted of a crime; and
- Aliens who obtain admissions or status by visa, identification, or immigration benefit fraud.

As you can see from the above priority list, ICE generally seeks to apprehend certain types of criminal aliens; particularly those aliens who have committed violent crimes or posed a danger to national security. But do not let this list deceive you. ICE constantly changes its priorities based on available resources and White House policies. When Barack Obama was the President of the United States, for example, his policy allowed ICE agents to apprehend aliens who had aggravated felonies, crimes of violence, or multiple misdemeanor convictions, while systematically ignoring other aliens who were illegally in the country. However, when Donald J. Trump became the U.S. president, his policy called for ICE agents to arrest and deport anyone that they found to be in the country illegally.

Still the priority list can be very useful to you. As with all decisions, the more information you have at your disposal, the better chance you have of making a favorable decision. Earlier in this chapter you learned about the person in Mississippi who was able to avoid federal prosecution. That was accomplished because his defense attorney learned ICE's current policies and convinced an ICE agent that it was in ICE's (and the country's) best interest to deport his client. Similarly, the person who was arrested by the Pittsburgh Police Department was released from the county jail after paying a fine for the public intoxication charge because he was a low priority to ICE officials at the time.

4. **<u>Reinstatement of Prior Order of Removal</u>**

In 1996, Congress passed the Illegal Immigration Reform and Immigration Responsibility Act of 1996 (IIRIRA). The provision of the law that is relevant to the discussions in this book is the allowance of an administrative reinstatement of prior deportation, exclusion, and removal orders.

Pursuant to INA §241(a)(5), ICE is authorized to reinstate a final order against an alien who has reentered the United States illegally after having been removed or having departed voluntarily while under an order of removal. The prior order of removal is reinstated from its original date and is not subject to being reopened or reviewed. Importantly, an alien can be removed under the prior order at any time after reentry into the United States.

This streamlined process allows an ERO officer to seek reinstatement of the prior order of removal without a lengthy hearing before an immigration judge. Basically, the officer, using available records such as the alien's A-file, confirms that the alien in question is the one for whom the prior removal order was issued and that the alien had been previously deported or removed. Once he or she completes this process, the agent creates a Record of Proceedings, with documentary evidence, to be presented to the deciding official such as field operation chief, supervisory special agent, or any other official authorized under law. Once this deciding official reviews and signs the I-871 form, reinstating the prior order, the ERO officer issues a new Warrant of Removal (I-205 form). This warrant allows immigration officials to take the alien into custody for subsequent deportation or removal.

According to ICE's Criminal Alien Program Handbook, "[r]einstatement does not preclude criminal prosecution ... Whenever possible, reinstatement processing should be completed before referring an alien for criminal prosecution. Aliens whose reinstatement processing is completed prior to criminal prosecution, will be removed more quickly after any criminal sentence is served."

As you can see there may be a period of time between the commencement of the reinstatement process and the presentation of the case to the U.S. Attorney's office for prosecution. You may be able to use this time period to your advantage, particularly if you are in pre-trial state custody. With reference to the Mississippi case described earlier in this chapter, the defense attorney was able to get the immigration official to forego federal prosecution in exchange for the defendant making a sworn statement about his prior deportation and subsequent illegal reentry into the U.S. This sworn statement allowed the ERO officer to more quickly obtain a new Warrant of Removal. All parties were happy with the outcome—which rarely happens in criminal cases.

This chapter was not intended to be a complete guide on criminal immigration laws. Rather, it was designed to give you a broad overview on how ICE personnel operate with regards to the apprehension, detention, and removal of criminal aliens. Because immigration laws are so complex and often change, I strongly recommend that you consult with a competent defense attorney who has a strong background in immigration law. If you are a criminal alien who has been arrested, you face possible severe consequences for both the underlying crime which led to your arrest and federal prosecution for returning to the U.S. illegally. As with the Mississippi case, a good defense attorney can lessen your exposure and produce a more favorable outcome.

CHAPTER 3
FEDERAL EARLY RELEASE PROGRAM

One of the easiest methods of seeking a reduced sentence is the federal early release program. It simply requires a federal non-U.S. citizen prisoner to send a letter to the U.S. Attorney General. That is not a misprint! I'll write it again. A federal non-U.S. citizen prisoner simply sends a letter to the Attorney General requesting to be let out of prison early. Does that sound too easy? It is not only easy; it works. And believe it or not, the process for some state prisoners, which will be discussed in the following chapters, is even easier.

Title 8, United States Code, section 1231(a)(4)(B)(i) reads, in part, that "[t]he Attorney General is authorized to remove an alien in accordance with applicable procedures under this Act before the alien has completed a sentence of imprisonment . . ."

If the alien is in federal custody and the U.S. Attorney General determines that: (1) the alien has not been convicted of a violent crime, a crime relating to smuggling or harboring of aliens, or one of the specific aggravated felonies listed under Title 8, United States Code, section 1101(a)(43); (2) the alien's conviction is final; and (3) the alien's removal is in the best interest of the United States, the Attorney General can grant early release to the alien. See Figure 3-1.

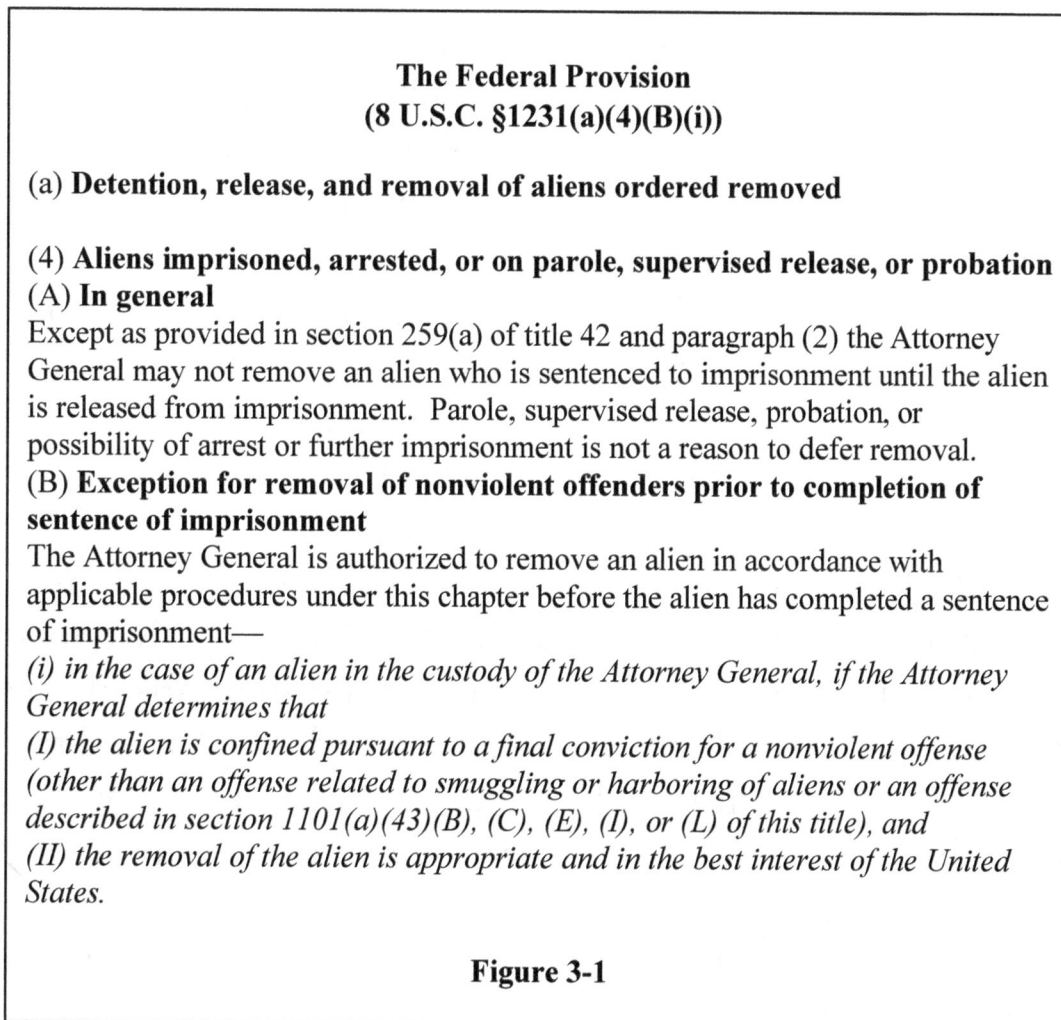

**The Federal Provision
(8 U.S.C. §1231(a)(4)(B)(i))**

(a) **Detention, release, and removal of aliens ordered removed**

(4) **Aliens imprisoned, arrested, or on parole, supervised release, or probation**
(A) **In general**
Except as provided in section 259(a) of title 42 and paragraph (2) the Attorney General may not remove an alien who is sentenced to imprisonment until the alien is released from imprisonment. Parole, supervised release, probation, or possibility of arrest or further imprisonment is not a reason to defer removal.
(B) **Exception for removal of nonviolent offenders prior to completion of sentence of imprisonment**
The Attorney General is authorized to remove an alien in accordance with applicable procedures under this chapter before the alien has completed a sentence of imprisonment—
(i) in the case of an alien in the custody of the Attorney General, if the Attorney General determines that
(I) the alien is confined pursuant to a final conviction for a nonviolent offense (other than an offense related to smuggling or harboring of aliens or an offense described in section 1101(a)(43)(B), (C), (E), (I), or (L) of this title), and
(II) the removal of the alien is appropriate and in the best interest of the United States.

Figure 3-1

Put simply, this statute gives the Attorney General the sole discretion to remove from the country before he or she completes his or her federal sentence any nonviolent non-U.S. citizen prisoner.

I learned about the federal program back in the early 2000s when a Mexican national named Miguel asked me to help him fill out the early release paperwork. At that time, an inmate could request the early release paperwork from his unit team, fill it out, and return it to his unit team. Weeks or months later, anyone who was granted relief would be called into the unit team office to sign a notification form, which informed the person that he or she had been granted early release and advised the person of the consequences if the person unlawfully returned to the United States. Miguel was one of the lucky ones who was granted early release. Therefore, the program definitely works. Moreover, it has worked for a number of years.

Awareness of the federal program has changed over the years. For instance, most current unit team members (counselors, case managers, and unit managers) are in the dark about the program. In fact, if you asked one of them about the program, you would undoubtedly receive a blank stare.

Yet BOP staff members are not the only ones who are in the dark. Several years ago I met a guy who had recently transferred from an Arizona state prison. While at the state prison, this guy had witnessed several state inmates who had filed for and received early release pursuant to federal and state law. This guy asked me to file the early release paperwork under the federal provision of the statute now that he was in the BOP's custody. I sent him to his unit team to get the early release paperwork. Each member of his unit team whom he spoke with did not know that alien inmates were eligible for early release. They each thought he was seeking a "treaty transfer," a totally different program that does not release a prisoner from incarceration. So I prepared an early release letter for him and had him send it to the Attorney General's office in Washington, D.C. Eric Holder was the Attorney General at the time. However, the person in the Attorney General's office who received the letter had no idea what it was. She thought that it was a Freedom of Information Act (FOIA) request seeking information about the Rapid REPAT program, the program for state inmates which was run by Immigration and Customs Enforcement (ICE) (More about this program in the next chapter). So she forwarded the letter to ICE. When that agency received the letter, it responded by letter to the prisoner and stated that it was unaware of any federal program that allowed for early release. Shortly after he received the letter from ICE, Loretta Lynch became the new Attorney General. I helped him re-send the early release letter to the Attorney General's office. Along with that letter, we enclosed a cover letter to Mrs. Lynch, which stated the purpose of the early release letter and which cited the Attorney General's discretionary authority to release from federal prison any nonviolent alien. Attorney General Lynch responded by letter, acknowledging her authority to reduce his sentence. She then sent a letter to the warden at the prison where the person was incarcerated. The letter asked for the warden's recommendation. The warden ultimately recommended that early release be denied because the guy had previously received an incident report involving the possession of a dangerous weapon. The Attorney General took the warden's recommendation into account and denied early release to the person.

Even though the person's early release was denied, the point is, there may be any number of individuals who profess ignorance about the program. However, as the above story shows, you must keep trying because the program is still alive and well.

I believe that the lack of knowledge about the federal program stems from two factors. First, the Attorney General has not developed a "formal" policy or procedure for federal inmates to follow, which in turn leads people to believe that federal prisoners cannot apply for early release under this law. For example, in November 2012, the National Immigration Project of the National Lawyers Guild developed a Practice Advisory which claimed that "[a] prisoner in federal custody cannot yet apply for deportation under the [statute] because the Attorney General has not, to date, implemented it."

While it is true that the Attorney General has not developed a "formal" federal policy, it is incorrect to state that federal prisoners cannot apply for early release under the law. In fact, in 2008, a federal prisoner filed a motion in the U.S. District Court for the Southern District of New York, asking the court to order the Attorney General to grant him early release. The district judge ruled that he lacked jurisdiction to grant the requested relief and denied the motion. The judge, however, directed the U.S. Attorney and BOP to provide letters outlining the procedure for seeking immigration early release.

As the U.S. Attorney's letter to the defendant and his attorney illustrated, there had long been an informal procedure for requesting early release and that any federal prisoner who meets the eligibility requirements can apply.

Second, there has been a significant increase in reduced sentences due to the early disposition program, also known as the "fast-track" program.

Fast-track programs originated around 1994 in the Southern District of California, where the number of illegal re-entry cases was overwhelming the capacity to prosecute violators. The United States Attorney for that district created a program that would recommend a 24-month sentence for defendants who violated

Title 8, United States Code, section 1326, in return for the defendants' waiver of various rights, to include indictment by grand jury, trial by jury, presentation of a pre-sentence report, and appellate review of the sentence. United States Attorneys in other districts, predominantly those along the United States southwestern border with Mexico, facing similar pressures, soon adopted their own programs, offering offenders an array of options, such as plea agreements to reduced sentences (by lowering the offense level) or to a lesser offense (e.g., entering the United States without inspection, in violation of Title 8, United States Code, section 1325).

In 2003, Congress expressly approved such programs in section 401(m)(2)(B) of the Prosecutorial Remedies and Other Tools to End the Exploitation of Children Today Act ("PROTECT Act"), which instructed the United States Sentencing Commission to issue a policy statement authorizing a downward departure "pursuant to an early disposition program authorized by the Attorney General." As directed by Congress, the Sentencing Commission adopted United States Sentencing Guideline (U.S.S.G.) section 5K3.1 ("Early Disposition Programs"), which provided that, "[u]pon motion of the Government, the court may depart downward not more than 4 levels pursuant to an early disposition program authorized by the Attorney General of the United States and the United States Attorney for the district in which the court resides." After the Sentencing Commission adopted section 5K3.1, the development of the fast-track program was prolific. Within a couple of years, the program was available in 13 of 94 federal districts. In those districts that did not initially have fast-track programs, defendants attempted to get similar treatment from the courts. They were generally denied a similar downward departure. However, on January 31, 2012, Deputy Attorney General James Cole issued a Department of Justice

Memorandum ("Memo") that reflected a change in policy that allowed for the use of fast-track programs in all districts and established uniform guidelines. The policy had an effective date of March 1, 2012. See Appendix A.

Based on that memo, the U.S. Attorneys in each of the districts developed fast-track programs. To date, there are still varying degrees of eligibility requirements within each of the districts. For example, in the Southern District of New York, the defendant must be charged solely with illegal re-entry in order to qualify for the fast-track program in that district. In the Western District of North Carolina, even if the person is charged solely with illegal re-entry, he or she may not be eligible for the fast-track program in that district if the person has a prior drug trafficking conviction. In California, where the program originated, defendants can get a fast-track downward departure even if they are charged with a crime other than illegal re-entry, such as drug trafficking.

The net result of the fast-track program is that defendants, especially those charged with illegal re-entry, generally get a reduction in their sentence at the time of their initial sentence. For that reason, many of these same defendants do not realize that they may also qualify for immigration early release.

Another result of the fast-track program is that the number of eligible people who have filed for immigration early release has dwindled to a trickle. This has caused the BOP staff and other federal government personnel to incorrectly assume that the program no longer exists. However, as the prior story showed, the program still exists.

There are some key differences between the fast-track program and immigration early release. The fast-track program is a pre-sentence program that allows the judge to reduce by up to four levels an alien's base offense level (known as a "downward departure"), but only after the U.S. Attorney's Office has filed a motion seeking such a reduction. On the other hand, the immigration early release program is a post-sentence program which does not require the U.S. Attorney's Office to file any motion on the alien's behalf. Generally, the fast-track reduction is awarded to aliens charged with illegal re-entry. There are a few exceptions, most notably in U.S. district courts in California, where the courts grant fast-track downward departures for various types of crimes. The alien's past criminal history usually does not play a part in determining whether the alien is eligible for the fast-track program. An immigration early release can be awarded to an alien who has violated a wide range of state and federal laws in his or her current case. In fact, it is easier to list the crimes that would make an alien ineligible for an immigration early release than to list those crimes that do not. If the alien is currently convicted of a "crime of violence," alien harboring and/or smuggling, illicit trafficking in a controlled substance, illicit trafficking in firearms or destructive devices, felon in possession of explosive material or firearms, child pornography, or any national defense violations, the alien may not be eligible for immigration early release. See Figure 3-2.

List of nonviolent crimes, under 8 U.S.C. §1101(a)(43), which make a *federal* prisoner ineligible for early release:

(B) illicit trafficking in a controlled substance

(C) illicit trafficking in firearms or destructive devices

(E) an offense described in —

- 18 U.S.C. §842(h) or (i)(relating to explosive material offenses);

- 18 U.S.C. §844(d), (e), (f), (g), (h), or (i)(relating to explosive material offenses);

- 18 U.S.C. §922(g)(1), (2), (3), (4), or (5)(relating to felon or alien in possession of a firearm);

- 18 U.S.C. §922(j), (n), (o), (p), or (r)(relating to firearm offenses);

- 18 U.S.C. §924(b) or (h)(relating to firearm offenses); or

- 26 U.S.C. §5861 (relating to firearm offenses)

(I) an offense described in —

- 18 U.S.C. §2251 (relating to sexual exploitation of children);

- 18 U.S.C. §2251A (relating to buying or selling children); or

- 18 U.S.C. §2252 (relating to child pornography)

(L) an offense described in —

- 18 U.S.C. §793 (relating to gathering or transmitting national defense information);

- 18 U.S.C. §798 (relating to disclosure of classified information);

- 18 U.S.C. §2153 (relating to sabotage);

- 18 U.S.C. §2381 (relating to treason);

- 18 U.S.C. §2381 (relating to misprision of treason); or

- 50 U.S.C. §421 (relating to protecting the identity of undercover intelligence or undercover agents).

Figure 3-2

If you have not yet been sentenced, you should seek a fast-track downward departure in your district, if you think you may be eligible.[2] If, on the other hand, you have already been sentenced, you should apply for an immigration early release (even if you did receive a fast-track downward departure).

As stated earlier, to seek an immigration early release, you need only send a letter to the Attorney General. This letter will generally be a recap of the positive things that you accomplished while in prison and an outline of your future goals.

Before you write the letter, you should get from your unit team an "Inmate Skills Development Plan" form. See Appendix B. This document has several different sections, which includes Personal Data, Sentencing Data, Financial Responsibility Data, Education Data, Work Data, Discipline History, and Medical Duty Status. The document begins by listing your name, register (inmate) number, security level, custody classification, projected release date, age, date of birth (DOB), and sex in the Personal Data section. In the example in Appendix B, the person scored as a medium security inmate who is designated with an "in" custody classification (which means the person must remain "behind the wall or double fence" at all times). The person's release date is October 22, 2031—if the person earns all of the good time credit that is available.

The next part of the document lists your Sentencing Data, to include your offense of conviction, length of sentence (to include any term of supervised release), the date your sentence began, the amount of time you have served thus far, any jail credit time you received, and the amount of good time credit that is available to you. The amount of time served and jail credit is important because it gives you an accurate picture of the exact amount of

---

[2] If you are not eligible for a fast-track downward departure and have not been sentenced, be sure to read the "Plea Agreement" section in Chapter 5.

time you have been incarcerated. In the example, the person has been incarcerated for 6 years, 8 months, and 17 days, while another 654 days (1 year, 289 days) was spent in county jail. The person is eligible to earn a total of 1176 days of good time credit during the course of serving his sentence.

Next, the Financial Responsibility Data section lists, among other things, any court-ordered assessment fees, restitution, and/or fines that you must pay. It also lists the name of the district court where you were convicted and any financial payment schedule you have agreed to. In the example, the person was ordered by the United States District Court for the Western District of Pennsylvania to pay $100 in court assessment fees. The person still owes $100 but has agreed to pay $25 per month to pay off the balance.

Another critical section in the document is the Education Data section. This section first lists whether you are proficient in the English language and whether you obtained your high school diploma or GED. Next, it lists each of the educational courses that you have completed while incarcerated, the date of completion, and the number of hours earned. The example shows that the person is proficient in English, has obtained his high school diploma, and has completed several educational courses, to include vocational trade (VT), adult continuing education (ACE), and pre-release preparation (RPP) classes.

The Work Data section comes immediately after the Education Data section, and provides a list of your current work assignment and the date on which you started your assignment. This section then lists any of your prior work assignments (Work History), the name of the prison where you worked, and the dates you started and stopped your prior work assignments. The example shows that the person started working as a unit based tutor on March 23, 2016. According to the document, he is still employed in that position. The example also shows that the person does not have any prior work assignments at any other facilities.

Yet another critical section in the document is the Discipline History section. This section highlights your disciplinary history. If you received an incident report, this section includes a list of whether you appeared before the UDC (Unit Disciplinary Committee) or the DHO (Discipline Hearing Officer), the date of your hearing, the incident report number, a description of the incident, and any sanctions that you may have received because of the incident.

The final section of the document is the Medical Duty Status Assignment section. If you have a medical condition that limits your work ability, this section may play an important role when you complete the immigration early release letter.

To be sure, the Inmate Skills Development Plan form has more sections than I have listed here. However, you most likely will not need the information contained in those sections to complete your letter to the Attorney General.

Okay, you have compiled the necessary paperwork to write your immigration early release letter to the Attorney General. The only thing left to do is write the letter. Before you begin, look at Figure 3-3(a), 3-3(b), and 3-3(c). Use the example letter as a guide to complete your own letter.

After you write the date and your name and address, you would write the name and address of the Attorney General. If at all possible, you want to use the name of the current Attorney General who is in office. If you are unsure of the person's name, ask your unit team or a staff member who works in the Education Department.

The "RE" section should contain the subject of the letter and your case citation (case name and case number). In the example in Figure 3-3(a), the subject of the letter is "Immigration Early

Release," while the case citation is "United States v. Miguel-Hernandez, Case No. 2:15-CR-0897-BTM."

November 5, 2017

Jorge A. Miguel-Hernandez
Reg. No. 08778-079
Federal Correctional Institution
P.O. Box 1000
Oxford, WI 53952

Jeff Sessions, Attorney General
Department of Justice
950 Pennsylvania Ave., N.W.
Washington, DC 20530

RE: Immigration Early Release Request
United States v. Miguel-Hernandez, Case No. 2:15-CR-0897-BTM

Dear Mr. Sessions:

This letter is a request for early release pursuant to Title 8, United States Code, section 1231(a)(4).

Under section 1231(a)(4)(B)(i), the Attorney General may remove "nonviolent offenders prior to completion of imprisonment . . . if the Attorney General determines that (I) the alien is confined pursuant to a final conviction for a nonviolent offense [or an offense listed under 8 U.S.C. section 1101 (a)(43)(B), (C), (E), (I), or (L)] and (II) the removal of the alien is appropriate and in the best interest of the United States."

I believe that I meet the above criteria. I am presently incarcerated at the Federal Correctional Institution in Oxford, Wisconsin. I was convicted on June 22, 2016 in the United States District Court for the Southern District of Texas for illegal re-entry. I was sentenced to 46 months of imprisonment. My conviction is final. My projected release date is October 20, 2019.

I came to the United States when I was 17 years old. During my stay in the United States I earned my General Equivalency Diploma (GED) in Hidalgo County, Texas. I completed a Class A driver's licensure program at the Southern

Figure 3-3(a)

Texas Community College. While I was at the community college, I met a young woman, who I began dating. After we graduated, we began living together.

We had our first child together in May 2010. I got a job as an over-the-road truck driver, a position I held for almost two years. Unfortunately, I was charged with and convicted of running a gambling operation. It was my first conviction. I served 18 months in state prison. After I was released, I was deported to Mexico.

I tried to get my son's mother to bring our son to visit me in Mexico, but she refused to visit. So I decided to return to the United States to visit my son. I was arrested by a police officer of the San Antonio Police Department and later turned over to federal authorities.

After I was sentenced, I was sent to the Federal Correctional Institution at Oxford. While at the facility, I enrolled in the Culinary Arts apprenticeship program. Upon completing the program, I was assigned to the Food Service Department as an officer's mess (OM) cook, preparing daily meals for the prison's staff. In addition to the Culinary Arts program, I completed the 7-Step Program, which helps inmates to think positively and constructively as they prepare for their release from prison, and the Victim Awareness Program. Moreover, I am pursuing my Associate's Degree in Business from Adams State University. I am on schedule to earn my degree next June. Importantly, I have never received any incident reports for prison rules violations and have great rapport with both staff and inmates.

My early release from prison and deportation to Mexico would be in the best interest of the United States because it would save the BOP more than $72,000. The annual cost of housing a person in a federal prison is $36,299.25 and I have about two years left on my federal sentence.

Further, I have never committed a violent crime. My first conviction was for a state gambling violation. In that case, I ran a BINGO contest one night to

Figure 3-3(b)

raise money for diabetes. That disease claimed the life of my grandmother in 2006. I raised $5,980, which I promptly turned over to the local chapter of the American Diabetes Association. However, I did not have a state license to run such an operation nor was I operating as a tax-exempt organization. This violated the state's gaming laws. I entered a guilty plea to the charge and served my time. My current offense is for illegal re-entry. I returned to the United States solely to visit my son. However, I will not have to return to the United States in the future because my son's mother (with our son) has been deported to Mexico. They currently live with my relatives in Mexico City. Moreover, I will be legally employed immediately upon my return to Mexico. My father purchased a food truck business that specializes in Southwest Texas cuisine. When I am released, I will serve as a Chef in one of the food trucks. Also, my father is paying for my business degree so that I can take over the food truck business after I have a few years of hands-on experience. Last year's gross revenue for his food truck business was $538,127.

For the reasons outlined in this letter, I respectfully request that you grant me early release and deport me to Mexico.

Respectfully,

Jorge A. Miguel-Hernandez

Enclosure: Inmate Skills Development Plan form and Certificates (5)

Figure 3-3(c)

The reason that you want to put the subject at the beginning of the letter is so that the person who receives it (most likely the Attorney General's secretary), can quickly see what the letter is about and make sure that it is properly routed to the correct person. Remember, the Department of Justice has thousands of employees and your letter could take many days to reach the proper person if it is not properly labeled.

Similarly, placing the case citation at the beginning of the letter allows the recipient to quickly look up your case rather than having to perform an exhaustive search through various files or computer records. You want to make things as easy as possible for the person. It will speed up the procedure because the person will be more likely to process an easy request than one that proves more difficult.

The next section talks about the Attorney General's authority to grant immigration early release. This is very important. The Attorney General may be a recent appointee who has never worked in the Justice Department. Therefore, he or she may not know the full extent of his or her authority. Or, the person, like Eric Holder, may have many years of experience; yet as the earlier story showed, his secretary did not know about the program and thus sent the letter to ICE. I, therefore, recommend that you copy the opening paragraph in the example in Figure 3-3(a) and place that paragraph at the beginning of your letter.

The next section highlights your present situation. It lists where you are currently incarcerated, the date on which you were convicted or sentenced, the name of the U.S. district court that sentenced you, the offense of conviction, the length of sentence, and your projected release date. All of this information is contained on your "Inmate Skills Development Plan" form.

The next thing that you want to do is describe your past history, to include any prior convictions, and other significant events. In the example, the person described how he originally came to the United States, what he accomplished while he was in the United States (earning his GED, getting his truck driver's certificate, and rearing a child), his prior state conviction for gambling, and his subsequent deportation.

In the subsequent section, you would describe each of the positive things that you have accomplished since your arrest. This list can include those things that you did before reaching federal prison. For example, you may have earned your GED or taken an anger management class while in county jail. You would list these types of accomplishments in your letter. In the example letter, the person listed his accomplishments as completing the Culinary Arts, 7-Step, and Victim Awareness programs; pursuing his college degree; working as a cook in the staff dining room; and receiving no incident reports.

In the final section, you should explain how your early release and deportation would be in the best interest of the United States. This section is very important. Under section 1231(a)(4)(B)(i), the Attorney General can only release from prison early: (1) a non-violent alien whose conviction is final and (2) whose "removal . . . is appropriate and in the best interest of the United States." The law is very specific. Any early release must be in the best interest of the United States.

There are a number of ways in which you can demonstrate that your early release would be in the best interest of the United States. The most obvious way is to show that it would save money for the federal government. Every other year the U.S. Justice Department releases a report showing how much money it costs to house a person in a federal prison for one year. Right now, that cost is more than $36,000 per year. See Appendix C. In the example letter, the person stated that his release would save the BOP a total of more than $72,000. This was based on the fact that he had approximately 2 years remaining on his sentence and the reported annual prison cost at that time was $36,299.25.

If you do not have the Justice Department's prison cost report, you can estimate the cost at $36,000 per year (or $3,000 per month). Using this method, if you have four years remaining on your sentence, you would calculate the savings at $144,000 ($36,000 per year x 4 years). If you have years and months remaining on your sentence or if you have less than one year remaining, you can use the monthly calculation. An example would be if a person has 10 months remaining on his sentence, the savings would be $30,000 ($3,000 per month x 10 months).

Saving money for the federal government, however, cannot be the only reason that you list to demonstrate that your early release would be in the best interest of the United States. In the example letter, the person listed several good reasons. First, he explained that he had never been convicted of a violent crime. Politicians, prosecutors, and judges are always concerned with releasing early from prison a violent criminal because they fear that the person will commit another violent crime, perhaps even kill someone. Therefore, the push has generally been to release "nonviolent" defendants. For instance, you cannot receive an immigration early release if your current crime is a "crime of violence." Thus, if you do not have any violent crimes in your past (or no prior convictions), you need to clearly state that fact in your letter.

Second, if you have a prior conviction and you believe that you have a valid reason for that conviction, you can explain that reason in this section as well. I have often met people in federal prison who were drug addicts or abusers. To support their drug addiction, they often sold drugs. This often became necessary because their drug addiction made it difficult for them to keep a job. While their actions were still criminal, their intent was vastly different than someone who commits a crime purely for the money. If you feel that you committed the crime for a "valid" reason—love, fear, addiction, etc.—you should explain that reason in your letter. In the example, the person described his prior state gambling conviction. He did not attempt to blame anyone else for his crime. He accepted responsibility. Yet he also gave more detail about what happened; which showed that his crime was more a result of ignorance of state law than an attempt to cause harm or commit a crime.

Similarly, you will want to explain your reason, if any, for your current conviction. In the example, the person stated that he came to the United States solely to visit his young son. Importantly, he explained why he will not have to do it in the future; namely, his son now lives in Mexico.

Third, one of the biggest reasons that people illegally come to the U.S. is to seek better economic opportunities. A person may come to the U.S., get a job, and send a portion of his or her earnings back to his or her home country. We have all met people like this. I met an Ecuadorian national when I was at U.S.P. Atwater, in California. This person was a head orderly and made about $80 per month. He also had a side hustle, "running a store," which brought in another $100 each month. This allowed him to send about $150 each month to his wife in Ecuador, which is a significant amount of money when you consider the cost of living in that country. The people in power understand that many people come to the U.S. for better economic opportunities. That knowledge is the reason that they sometimes do not seek the deportation of a person who is in the U.S. illegally, unless the person commits another type of crime. If you are seeking an immigration early release, however, you must show the Attorney General that you do not have to return to the U.S. for economical reasons. This can be done by showing that you have a job lined up in your home country. In the example, the person stated that he will work in his father's food truck business. He also showed how his current prison job (cook) and educational pursuit (earning a business degree) fits in with his future employment plans. This shows the Attorney General that the person is more likely to succeed. If you have a job waiting for you, you will want to be as specific as possible about the job. Better yet, you should get a letter from your potential employer and attach that letter to your letter to the Attorney General.

The above advice is designed to help you complete your immigration early release letter to the Attorney General. As stated earlier, you can use the example letter as a guide, but you do not have to follow it exactly since your circumstances will be different than those discussed in the example letter. Nevertheless, there are critical things that you will want to include in your letter. As the book recommended earlier, you will want to include the language about the Attorney General's authority to grant you early release from prison. If you do not have any violent crimes in your past, you will want to highlight that as well. Lastly, you must show how your early release will be a benefit to the United States.

After you have written your letter, you should copy your Inmate Skills Development Plan form, educational certificates, and the letter from your future employer, if any. You would place this material into a large envelope and mail it directly to the Attorney General's office. Preferably, you should send the envelope and its contents by certified mail and place it in the prison's legal mail system to ensure that you have a record of the fact that it made it to the Attorney General's office.

APPENDIX A
("FAST-TRACK" MEMORANDUM)

U.S. Department of Justice

Office of the Deputy Attorney General

The Deputy Attorney General

Washington, D.C. 20530

January 31, 2012

MEMORANDUM FOR ALL UNITED STATES ATTORNEYS

FROM: James M. Cole
            Deputy Attorney General

SUBJECT: Department Policy on Early Disposition or "Fast-Track" Programs

I. INTRODUCTION

In the 1990s, United States Attorneys' Offices and the Department developed early disposition or "fast-track" programs as a matter of prosecutorial discretion to handle increasingly large numbers of criminal immigration cases arising along the southwestern border of the United States. The Prosecutorial Remedies and Other Tools to End the Exploitation of Children Today Act ("PROTECT Act"), Pub. L. No. 108-066, 117 Stat. 650, Apr. 30, 2003, harmonized these programs with the departure provisions of the federal Sentencing Guidelines. More specifically, the PROTECT Act directed the Sentencing Commission to promulgate a statement by October 27, 2003, authorizing downward sentence departures of no more than four levels as part of an early disposition program authorized by the Attorney General and the United States Attorney. *See* Pub. L. No. 108-21, § 401(m)(2)(B), 117 Stat. 650, 675 (2003).[1]

This memorandum sets forth the revised policy and criteria for fast-track programs. It provides only internal Department of Justice guidance. It is not intended to, does not, and may not be relied upon to create any rights, substantive or procedural, enforceable at law by any party in any matter civil or criminal, nor does it place any limitations on otherwise lawful litigative prerogatives of the Department.

II. REVISED FAST-TRACK POLICIES

As stated above, fast-track programs originated in southwestern border districts with an exceptional volume of immigration cases. They are based on the premise that a defendant who promptly agrees to participate in such a program saves the government significant and scarce resources that can be used to prosecute other defendants, and that a defendant who receives a fast-track departure has demonstrated an acceptance of responsibility above and beyond what is already taken into account by the adjustments contained in the Sentencing Guidelines. In that context, these programs address a compelling, and otherwise potentially intractable, resource issue. Indeed, the need for fast-track programs has persisted and, in some districts, intensified.

---

[1] The requirement that a fast-track program be approved by the Attorney General can be satisfied by obtaining the approval of the Deputy Attorney General. *See* 28 U.S.C. § 510; 28 C.F.R. § 0.15(a).

On September 22, 2003, then-Attorney General Ashcroft issued a memorandum setting forth the criteria to be used by United States Attorneys' offices (USAOs) seeking to establish fast-track programs.[2] Since this memorandum was issued, the legal and operational circumstances surrounding fast-track programs have changed. Fast-track programs are no longer limited to the southwestern border districts; rather, some, but not all, non-border districts have sought and received authorization to implement fast-track programs. The existence of these programs in some, but not all, districts has generated a concern that defendants are being treated differently depending on where in the United States they are charged and sentenced.

In addition, the Sentencing Guidelines are no longer mandatory,[3] and federal courts of appeals are divided on whether a sentencing court in a non-fast-track district may vary downwards from the Guidelines range to reflect disparities with defendants who are eligible to receive a fast-track sentencing discount.[4] Because of this circuit conflict, USAOs in non-fast-track districts routinely face motions for variances based on fast-track programs in other districts. Courts that grant such variances are left to impose sentences that introduce additional sentencing disparities.

In light of these circumstances, the Department conducted an internal review of authorized fast-track programs. After consultation with the United States Attorneys in both affected and non-affected districts, the Department is revising its fast-track policy and establishing uniform, baseline eligibility requirements for any defendant who qualifies for fast-track treatment, regardless of where that defendant is prosecuted. This outcome is consistent with the Department's position on the Sentencing Guidelines as a means to achieve reasonable sentencing uniformity, and with Attorney General Holder's memorandum on charging and sentencing, which states that persons who commit similar crimes and have similar culpability should, to the extent possible, be treated similarly.[5] This policy does not, however, alter the criteria for prosecutorial discretion on whether to charge a particular defendant, nor does it require prosecuting additional cases.

---

[2] Memorandum from Attorney General John Ashcroft, *Department Principles for Implementing an Expedited Disposition or "Fast-Track" Prosecution Program in a District* (Sept. 22, 2003), *available at* http://10.173.2.12/jmd/lib/memo3.pdf.

[3] *United States v. Booker*, 543 U.S. 220 (2005).

[4] *Compare United States v. Gonzales-Zotelo*, 556 F.3d 736, 740-41 (9th Cir. 2009); *United States v. Vega-Castillo*, 540 F.3d 1235, 1238-39 (11th Cir. 2008); *United States v. Gomez-Herrera*, 523 F.3d 554, 559-64 (5th Cir. 2008) (holding that sentencing disparity resulting from fast-track programs is not "unwarranted") *with United States v. Lopez-Macias*, – F.3d –, 2011 WL 5310622 (10th Cir.); *United States v. Jimenez-Perez*, 659 F.3d 704 (8th Cir. 2011); *United States v. Reyes-Hernandez*, 624 F.3d 405, 417-18 (7th Cir. 2010); *United States v. Camacho-Arellano*, 614 F.3d 244, 249-50 (6th Cir. 2010); *United States v. Arrelucea-Zamudio*, 581 F.3d 142, 149-56 (3d Cir. 2009); *United States v. Rodriguez*, 527 F.3d 221, 226-31 (1st Cir. 2008) (holding that sentencing courts can consider the disparity created by fast-track programs).

[5] Memorandum from Attorney General Eric H. Holder, Jr., *Department Policy on Charging and Sentencing* (May 19, 2010). This memorandum notes that it does not "impact the guidance provided in the September 22, 2003 memorandum and elsewhere regarding 'fast-track' programs. In those districts where an approved 'fast-track' program has been established, charging decisions and disposition of charges must comply with the Department's requirements for that program." Pursuant to today's memorandum, the guidance provided in the September 22, 2003 memorandum regarding fast-track programs is superseded.

The Early Release Provision / David Mathis

III. NEW REQUIREMENTS GOVERNING UNITED STATES ATTORNEY IMPLEMENTATION OF ILLEGAL REENTRY FAST-TRACK PROGRAMS

Districts prosecuting felony illegal reentry cases (8 U.S.C. § 1326)—the largest category of cases authorized for fast-track treatment—shall implement an early disposition program in accordance with the following requirements and the exercise of prosecutorial discretion by the United States Attorney:

A. *Defendant Eligibility.* The United States Attorney retains the discretion to limit or deny a defendant's participation in a fast-track program based on—

(1) The defendant's prior violent felony convictions (including murder, kidnapping, voluntary manslaughter, forcible sex offenses, child-sex offenses, drug trafficking, firearms offenses, or convictions which otherwise reflect a history of serious violent crime);

(2) The defendant's number of prior deportations, prior convictions for illegal reentry under 8 U.S.C. § 1326, prior convictions for other immigration-related offenses, or prior participation in a fast-track program;

(3) If the defendant is part of an independent federal criminal investigation, or if he or she is under any form of court or correctional supervision; or

(4) With supervisory approval, circumstances at the time of the defendant's arrest or any other aggravating factors identified by the United States Attorney.

B. *Expedited Disposition.* Within 30 days from the defendant being taken into custody on federal criminal charges, absent exceptional circumstances such as the denial of adequate assistance of counsel or a substantial delay in necessary administrative procedures, the defendant must agree to enter into a plea agreement consistent with the requirements of Section C, below.

C. *Minimum Requirements for "Fast-Track" Plea Agreement.* The defendant must enter into a written plea agreement that includes at least the following items—

(1) The defendant agrees to a factual basis that accurately reflects his or her offense conduct and stipulates to the facts related to the prior conviction and removal;

(2) The defendant agrees not to file any of the motions described in Rules 12(b)(3), Fed. R. Crim. P.;

(3) As determined by the United States Attorney after taking into account applicable law and local district court practice and policy, the defendant agrees to waive the right to argue for a variance under 18 U.S.C. § 3553(a), and to waive

appeal and the opportunity to challenge his or her conviction under 28 U.S.C. § 2255, except on the issue of ineffective assistance of counsel; and

(4) The United States Attorney shall retain discretion to impose additional procedural requirements for fast-track plea agreements; specifically, the United States Attorney has discretion to require that the defendant agree to enter into a sentencing agreement pursuant to Fed. R. Crim. P. 11(c)(1)(C), and/or to waive a full pre-sentence investigation as conditions of participation.

D.   *Additional Provisions of a Plea Agreement.* If the above conditions are satisfied—including those imposed at the discretion of the United States Attorney as provided for in Section C(4)—the attorney for the Government shall move at sentencing pursuant to Sentencing Guidelines Section 5K3.1 for a downward departure from the adjusted base offense level found by the District Court (after application of the adjustment for acceptance of responsibility) as follows:

Four levels for all defendants, except those with a criminal history category VI or with at least one felony conviction for a serious violent offense. For the latter category, if the defendant is not excluded under Section A(1), the government may only offer a two-level departure, with supervisory approval and on a case-by-case basis after considering the interest of public safety.

Districts prosecuting felony illegal reentry cases should implement this new policy no later than by March 1, 2012.[6] This will provide any needed transition, especially for those districts without fast-track programs currently in place.

cc: The Attorney General
      The Associate Attorney General
      The Solicitor General
      The Assistant Attorney General, Criminal Division
      The Director, Executive Office for United States Attorneys

---

[6] In the interim, authorization for illegal reentry fast-track programs in districts which already have such programs in place is extended to March 1, 2012. Further, the Department has authorized fast-track programs for offenses other than felony illegal reentry. These other programs will continue to be authorized until March 1, 2012. This extension will allow for a substantive review of these programs in due course.

APPENDIX B
(INMATE SKILLS DEVELOPMENT PLAN FORM)

Page 2

Department of Justice
INMATE SKILLS DEVELOPMENT PLAN PROGRAM REVIEW: 09-26-2016
Federal Bureau of Prisons

Financial Plan		Comm Dep-6 mos:	$825.09
Active:	Y	Commissary:	
Financial Plan Date: 09-26-2016		Balance:	$168.22

Payments

| Commensurate: | Y |
| Missed: | N |

Judicial Recommendations: NONE / / FRP / NONE

Special Conditions of Supervision: SEE J&C

USPO	Belinda M. Ashley, Chief	[POC]
Sentencing:	Pennsylvania Western Probation Office	Relocation: [District]
	United States Post Office and Courthouse	[Street Address/Suite]
	700 Grant Street Room 3330	[City], [State] [Zip]
	Pittsburgh, PA 15219-5219	[Phone]/[Fax]
Phone/Fax:	412-395-6907 / 412-395-4854	

Subject to 18 U.S.C. 4042(B) Notification: Y   DNA Required: Y
- Past conviction for a crime of violence (state and   Treaty Transfer Case: N
federal)
- Current conviction for a crime of violence (state and
federal)

Profile Comments:

EDUCATION DATA

Facility	Assignment	Description	Start Date	Stop Date
HER	ESL HAS	ENGLISH PROFICIENT	04-20-1995	CURRENT
HER	GED HAS	COMPLETED GED OR HS DIPLOMA	04-10-1995	CURRENT

COMPLETED EDUCATION/COURSES

Course Description	Completion Date	Course Hours
VT ADVANCED COMPUTERS	09-21-2016	110
ACE NUTRITION & MEALS (RPP 1)	07-26-2016	2
VT COMPUTER (RPP2)	06-16-2016	110
ACE INTRO TO BUDGETING (RPP 3)	06-03-2016	2
ACE MANNERS FOR MEN (RPP 6)	06-03-2016	2
ACE JOB INTERVIEWING (RPP 2)	05-18-2016	2
CREDIT EVAL AND REPAIR (RPP 3)	05-06-2016	2
ACE TIME MANAGEMENT (RPP 6)	04-28-2016	2
ACE DRESS FOR SUCCESS (RPP 6)	04-21-2016	2
RESUME WRITING 101 (RPP 2)	04-07-2016	2
ACE BUSINESS ETIQUETTE	01-27-2016	2

Generated: 09-26-2016 13:18:20   Page 2   Inmate Copy ISDS Version: 1.6.2d

---

Department of Justice
INMATE SKILLS DEVELOPMENT PLAN Current Program Review: 09-26-2016
Federal Bureau of Prisons

Name:		Institution:	HERLONG FCI
Register Number:			P.O. BOX 900
Security/Custody:	MEDIUM/IN		HERLONG, CA 95113
Projected Release:	10-22-2031 / GCT REL	Telephone:	(530) 827-6000

Next Review Date:	10-31-2016	Driver's License/State:	/
Next Custody Review Date:	05-05-2017	FBI Number:	
Age/DOB/Sex:	52 / 02-12-1964 / M	DCDC Number:	
CIM Status:	Y	INS Number:	
	If yes, reconciled: Y	PDID Number:	
		Other IDs:	

Release Residence:	[POC]	Release Employer:	[Name]
			[Address]
		Contact	[POC]
Telephone:	[Phone]	Telephone:	

| Primary Emergency Contact: | | Secondary Emergency Contact: | |

| Telephone: | | Telephone: | |

Mentor Information:

Controlling Sentence Information:

Offense(s)/Violator Offenses:				

	Sentence	Sentencing Procedure	Supervision Term
	300 MONTHS	3559 PLRA SENTENCE	5 YEARS

Controlling Sentence Began	Time Served/Jail Credit/Inoperative Time	Days GCT/EGT/SGT	Days FSGT/WSGT/OGGT	Parole Status
10-26-2011	6 YEARS 8 MONTHS 17 DAYS / 654 / 0	1176 / 0 / 0	0 / 0 / 0	NOT ENTERED
			Hearing Date:	
			Hearing Type:	
			Last USPC Action:	

Detainers: N

Special Parole Term: NOT ENTERED
Pending Charges: Yes-10-3-11, ASSAULT BY PRISONER,
AGGRAVATED ASSAULT, &
TERRORISTIC THREATS

CIM Status: Y   CIM Reconciled: Y

Financial Responsibility

	Imposed	Balance	Case No/Court of Jurisdiction	Assign/Schedule Payment
ASSESSMENT USDC	$100.00	$100.00	CR 10-19 WESTERN DISTRICT OF PENNSYLVANIA	FINANC RESP-PARTICIPATES $25.00 MONTHLY

Generated: 09-26-2016 13:18:20   Page 1   Inmate Copy ISDS Version: 1.6.2d

Department of Justice
Federal Bureau of Prisons:
INMATE SKILLS DEVELOPMENT PLAN   PROGRAM REVIEW: 09-26-2016

Inmate has no movement history items in this area

CASE MANAGEMENT ASSIGNMENTS

Facility	Assignment	Description	Start Date	Stop Date
HER	RPP COMPLT	RELEASE PREP PGM COMPLETE	09-17-2013	CURRENT
HER	V94 PV	V94 PAST VIOLENCE	12-07-2011	CURRENT
HER	V94 CVA913	V94 CURR VIOL ON/AFTER 91394	12-07-2011	CURRENT

MEDICAL DUTY STATUS ASSIGNMENTS

Facility	Assignment	Description	Start Date	Stop Date
HER	REG DUTY	NO MEDICAL RESTR--REGULAR DUTY	12-08-2011	CURRENT
HER	YES F/S	CLEARED FOR FOOD SERVICE	10-29-2003	CURRENT

Generated: 09-26-2016 13:18:20   Inmate Copy ISDS Version: 1.6.2d

---

Name: Reg No.

ACE BUSINESS ETIQUETTE	11-22-2014	2
ACE TIME MANAGEMENT	11-12-2014	2
BUSINESS OWNERSHIP (RPP3)	07-22-2014	16
FINANCIAL SEMINAR (RPP 3)	12-11-2013	2
(RPP 6) EMPLOYABLE LIFE SKILLS	09-17-2013	1
RELEASE PROCEDURES (RPP5)	09-17-2013	1
US PROBATION OFFICE (RPP4)	09-17-2013	1
CONSUMER CREDIT (RPP3)	09-17-2013	1
FGI EMPLOYMENT SKILLS (RPP2)	09-17-2013	1
HEALTH SERVICES	09-18-2013	20
BASIC ESSAY WRITING	05-29-2013	20
SPANISH 1 (RPP5)	05-05-2013	18
(RPP 6) DOING TIME WORKSHOP	10-02-2012	12
PARENTING BY HEART DVD	10-12-2012	2
RPP JOB SEARCH SKILLS	08-07-2012	14
PARENTING BY HEART DVD		

HIGH TEST SCORES

Test	Subtest	Score	Test Date	Test Fac	Form	Suite
Inmate has no score history items in this area						

WORK DATA

Facility	Assignment	Description	Start Date	Stop Date
HER	TUTOR S-A	UNIT BASE TUTOR-SIERRA A POD	03-23-2016	CURRENT

WORK HISTORY

Facility	Assignment	Work Assignment Description	Start Date	Stop Date
Inmate has no work history items in this area				

DISC PUNISH HISTORY

UDC/DHO	Hearing Date	Report No.	Prohibited Act/Description	Sanction
Inmate has no disciplinary history items in this area				

MOVEMENT DATA

Facility	Assignment	Description	Start Date	Stop Date
HER	A-DES	DESIGNATED, AT ASSIGNED FACIL	12-27-2012	CURRENT

MOVEMENT HISTORY

Facility	Assignment		Start Date	Stop Date

Generated: 09-26-2016 13:18:20   Inmate Copy ISDS Version: 1.6.2d

58

APPENDIX C
(AVERAGE COST OF INCARCERATION FORM)

Federal Register / Vol. 83, No. 83 / Monday, April 30, 2018 / Notices   18863

from current operations, and changes that did occur would be on an as-needed basis. Management of park visitors would continue to vary seasonally as visitor demand and needs change with many management strategies focusing on the peak season between mid-May and mid-October. Parking would remain available to all users on a first-come, first-served basis and right lane parking on the Park Loop Road would continue to occur. Temporary or permanent closures of roads and parking areas may occur if necessary to address safety and security concerns or to ensure the financial sustainability of the overall transportation system.

Alternative B—would establish a reservation system for parking at five of the primary attractions and trailheads along Park Loop Road during peak times and seasons, and eliminate right lane parking to improve traffic flows. Gates and queuing lanes would be constructed where needed to validate reservations and to control access on some first-come, first-served lots.

Alternative C: Proposed action and preferred alternative—would address transportation and congestion issues by establishing a reservation system for the Ocean Drive corridor, Cadillac Mountain Road, and the Jordan Pond North Lot during peak use season (approximately mid-May to mid-October). During initial implementation of this alternative, all other parking lots in the park would continue to be managed on a first-come, first-served basis; but the alternative includes an adaptive management strategy that directs park managers to monitor traffic and resource conditions elsewhere in the park. If monitoring indicates traffic or resource conditions worsening beyond established thresholds, access to Island Explorer routes entering the park, vehicle access to other parking lots, or vehicle access to the entire Park Loop Road may be added to the reservation systems. Expanded opportunities for parking and associated visitor access to the park (without private vehicles) would be provided via expanded public transit service and improvements at Hulls Cove and the Acadia Gateway Center.

Alternative D—would establish a systemwide approach to manage volume of vehicles on Park Loop Road during the peak use season. Gates and additional entrance stations would be installed at all access points to Park Loop Road and a timed-entry reservation system would be established for vehicle access to Park Loop Road during the peak use season. Once a visitor passes through ʴ entrance

station or gate during their reserved entry window, all parking lots on Park Loop Road would be available on a first-come, first-served basis.

Under all of the action alternatives (alternatives B, C, and D), vehicle size limits would be phased in for all commercial and noncommercial vehicles on the Park Loop Road to improve safety and maintain the historic character of the road. Also common to these alternatives, the number of oversize commercial vehicles (vehicles that do not fit within a standard parking space such as a bus) allowed at key locations at one time would be managed to ensure desired conditions are maintained and visitor capacities at the parks primary attractions are not exceeded.

The NPS will accept comments on the Draft Plan/EIS for a period of 60 days following publication of the Environmental Protection Agency's (EPA) Notice of Availability of the Draft Plan/EIS in the **Federal Register**. After the EPA Notice of Availability is published, the NPS will schedule public meetings to be held during the comment period. The comment period and dates, times, and locations of these public meetings will be announced through social media and local media outlets; and on the NPS Planning, Environment, and Public Comment website at *http://parkplanning.nps.gov/ACADTransportationPlan*, and Acadia National Park's website at *https://www.nps.gov/acad/index.htm*.

If you wish to comment, you may submit your comments by any one of several methods. The preferred method of commenting is to enter comments electronically through the PEPC website at *http://parkplanning.nps.gov/ACADTransportationPlan*. Comments will also be accepted in hardcopy by mail to: Acadia National Park, Attn: Transportation Plan, P.O. Box 177, Bar Harbor, ME 04609, or you may hand-deliver hardcopy comments to the park at 20 McFarland Hill Drive, Bar Harbor, ME. Comments will not be accepted in any other format beyond those specified above.

Before including your address, phone number, email address, or other personal identifying information in any comment, you should be aware that your entire comment—including your personal identifying information—may be made publicly available at any time. While you can ask us in your comment to withhold your personal identifying information from public review, we cannot guarantee that we will be able to do so.

Dated: March 13, 2018.

Deborah L. Conway,
Acting Regional Director, Northeast Region, National Park Service.
[FR Doc. 2018–08998 Filed 4–27–18; 8:45 am]
BILLING CODE 4312–52–P

DEPARTMENT OF JUSTICE

Bureau of Prisons

Annual Determination of Average Cost of Incarceration

AGENCY: Bureau of Prisons, Justice.
ACTION: Notice.

SUMMARY: This Notice publishes the annual determination of average cost of incarceration for the Fiscal Years (FY) 2016 and 2017. The fee to cover the average cost of incarceration for Federal inmates was $34,704.12 ($94.82 per day) in FY 2016 and $36,299.25 ($99.45 per day) in FY 2017. The average annual cost to confine an inmate in a Residential Re-entry Center was $29,166.54 ($79.69 per day) for FY 2016 and $32,309.80 ($88.52 per day) for FY 2017.

DATES: Applicable Date: April 30, 2018.

ADDRESSES: Office of General Counsel, Federal Bureau of Prisons, 320 First St. NW, Washington, DC 20534.

FOR FURTHER INFORMATION CONTACT: Sarah Qureshi, (202) 353–8248.

SUPPLEMENTARY INFORMATION:
Title 28 of the Code of Federal Regulations, part 505, allows for assessment and collection of a fee to cover the average cost of incarceration for Federal inmates. Under § 505.2, this fee is calculated by dividing the number representing Bureau of Prisons (Bureau) facilities' monetary obligation (excluding activation costs) by the number of inmate-days incurred for the preceding fiscal year, and then by multiplying the quotient by the number of days in the fiscal year.

Based on FY 2016 and FY 2017 data, the fee to cover the average cost of incarceration for Federal inmates was $34,704.12 ($94.82 per day) in FY 2016 and $36,299.25 ($99.45 per day) in FY 2017. The average annual cost to confine an inmate in a Residential Re-entry Center was $29,166.54 ($79.69 per day) for FY 2016 and $32,309.80 ($88.52 per day) for FY 2017. [Note: There were 366 days in FY 2016 and 365 days in FY 2017.)

Ken Hyle,
General Counsel, Federal Bureau of Prisons.
[FR Doc. 2018–09062 Filed 4–27–18; 8:45 am]
BILLING CODE 4410–05–P

Chapter 4
Rapid Removal of Eligible Parolees Accepted for Transfer (Rapid REPAT)

As previously mentioned, the procedure for some state non-U.S. citizen prisoners to seek immigration early release is even easier than the federal procedure. However, before we look at that procedure, let us review the federal statute (law) that gives the U.S. Attorney General the authority to grant early release to state non-U.S. citizen prisoners and to transport them to their home countries.

Title 8, United States Code, section 1231(a)(4)(B)(ii) reads, in part, that "[t]he [U.S.] Attorney General is authorized to remove an alien . . . before the alien has completed a [state] sentence of imprisonment . . . if the chief State official . . . determines that (I) the alien is confined pursuant to a final conviction for a nonviolent offense (other than an offense described in section 1101(a)(43)(C) or (E)); (II) the removal is appropriate and in the best interest of the state; and (III) submits a written request to the [U.S.] Attorney General that such alien be so removed." See Figure 4-1.

If you compare the federal and state provisions, you should notice some key differences between them. First, the removal of the state prisoner must be in the best interest of the state rather than the United States, as required of federal alien prisoners. Second, it is the "chief State official" who sends the written request or letter to the Attorney General, not the prisoner as required under the federal procedure. Here, the term "chief State official" means state or U.S. territory governor or his or her designated representative. Third, and perhaps most importantly, the list of crimes that preclude a state non-U.S. citizen prisoner from qualifying for early release is much shorter than the list under the federal procedure. The state prisoner in most cases, like the federal prisoner, must be currently convicted of a "nonviolent" crime to be eligible. However, there is a category of nonviolent crimes that may make a state non-U.S. citizen prisoner ineligible for immigration early release. That special category deals mainly with firearms, destructive devices, and/or explosives.

The State Provision
(8 U.S.C. §1231(a)(4)(B)(ii))

(a) Detention, release, and removal of aliens ordered removed

(4) Aliens imprisoned, arrested, or on parole, supervised release, or probation
(A) In general
Except as provided in section 259(a) of title 42 and paragraph (2) the Attorney General may not remove an alien who is sentenced to imprisonment until the alien is released from imprisonment. Parole, supervised release, probation, or possibility of arrest or further imprisonment is not a reason to defer removal.
(B) Exception for removal of nonviolent offenders prior to completion of sentence of imprisonment
The Attorney General is authorized to remove an alien in accordance with applicable procedures under this chapter before the alien has completed a sentence of imprisonment—
(ii) in the case of an alien in the custody of a State (or a political subdivision of a State), if the chief State official exercising authority with respect to the incarceration of the alien determines that
(I) the alien is confined pursuant to a final conviction for a nonviolent offense (other than an offense described in section 1101(a)(43)(C) or (E) of this title),
(II) the removal is appropriate and in the best interest of the State, and
(III) submits a written request to the Attorney General that such alien be so removed.

Figure 4-1

Section 1231(a)(4)(B)(ii) states that a person convicted of a crime listed in section 1101(a)(43)(C) or 1101(a)(43)(E) of Title 8 is ineligible for immigration early release. And while the crimes listed in section 1101(a)(43) are federal crimes, a state non-U.S. citizen prisoner may be ineligible for immigration early release if he or she was convicted of a similar state law. For example, Title 18, United States Code, section 922(g) makes it a federal crime for anyone who has been previously convicted of a felony to possess a firearm. This crime is listed in section 1101(a)(43). Each state also has a similar law that prohibits a felon from possessing a firearm. Therefore, a person convicted under a state's felon-in-possession law may be ineligible for immigration early release. You should read the accompanying box for a list of crimes found in section 1101(a)(43)(C) or (E), which would make a state prisoner ineligible for immigration early release. See Figure 4-2.

List of nonviolent crimes, under 8 U.S.C. §1101(a)(43), which make a *state* prisoner ineligible for early release:

(C) illicit trafficking in firearms or destructive devices
(E) an offense described in —

- 18 U.S.C. §842(h) or (i)(relating to explosive material offenses);
- 18 U.S.C. §844(d), (e), (f), (g), (h), or (i)(relating to explosive material offenses);
- 18 U.S.C. §922(g)(1), (2), (3), (4), or (5)(relating to felon or alien in possession of a firearm);
- 18 U.S.C. §922(j), (n), (o), (p), or (r)(relating to firearm offenses);
- 18 U.S.C. §924(b) or (h)(relating to firearm offenses); or
- 26 U.S.C. §5861 (relating to firearm offenses)

Figure 4-2

While Figure 4-2 lists those types of convictions that, under federal law, make a state non-U.S. citizen prisoner ineligible for immigration early release, states can and do develop their own eligibility requirements. For example, to be eligible for immigration early release in New Hampshire, a state prisoner must: (1) receive a final deportation order from ICE; (2) serve at least 1/3 of his or her minimum sentence; (3) not be convicted of a violent, sexual, or obstruction of justice offense; and (4) not be sentenced to an extended term of imprisonment under N.H. law. See Figure 4-3. See also Appendix G. Similarly, in Arizona, a state prisoner faces similar eligibility requirements, except that he or she must complete at least 1/2 of his or her sentence.

New Hampshire Revised Statute Annotated 651:25, VII

VII.(a) The commissioner of corrections may release a prisoner who is serving a New Hampshire state sentence to the custody and control of the United States Immigration and Customs Enforcement if all of the following requirements are satisfied:

(1) The department of corrections receives an order of deportation for the prisoner from the United States Immigration and Customs Enforcement;

(2) The prisoner has served at least 1/3 of the minimum sentences imposed by the court;

(3) The prisoner was not convicted of a violent crime, or any crime of obstruction of justice, or sentenced to an extended term of imprisonment under RSA 651:6; and

(4) The prisoner was not convicted of a sexual offense as defined in RSA 651-B:1, V.

(b) If a prisoner who is released from his or her state sentence pursuant to this section returns illegally to the United States, on notification from any federal or state law enforcement agency that the prisoner is in custody, the commissioner of corrections shall revoke the prisoner's release and immediately file a detainer seeking the prisoner's return to the custody of the department of corrections to serve the remainder of his or her sentence.

Figure 4-3

There are exceptions to the "nonviolent" crime rule. In the state of New York, for instance, if the person has not yet reached his or her parole eligibility date, he or she may be released early under the state's "Early Conditional Parole for Deportation Only" (ECPDO) program, if the person has not been convicted of one of the violent crimes listed under state law. However, if the person has reached his or her parole eligibility date, he or she may be released early under the state's "Conditional Parole for Deportation Only" (CPDO) program regardless of the nature of the conviction.

You have reviewed the federal law that governs early release for state non-U.S. citizen prisoners and found that there are three essential provisions. First, the state prisoner usually must have been convicted of a nonviolent offense. Second, the person's removal must be in the best interest of the state. Finally, state officials must submit a written request to the U.S. Attorney General.

Now, here is how state procedure is easier for most state prisoners than federal procedure is for federal prisoners. State procedures can be divided into two broad categories.

The first category is the Rapid Removal of Eligible Parolees Accepted for Transfer (Rapid REPAT) program. To handle the influx of state non-U.S. citizen prisoners (and to reduce the number of individual requests to the U.S. Attorney General), the federal government developed the Rapid REPAT program. This program, which is run by ICE, is a joint partnership between ICE and state correctional/parole agencies that allow for the early release of non-violent state prisoners who have final orders of removal from the United States. See Appendix D for Rapid REPAT Fact Sheet. Under the Rapid REPAT program, a non-U.S. citizen incarcerated in state prison may receive early "conditional" release if the prisoner agrees not to return to the

United States and waives his or her appeal rights associated with the prisoner's state conviction.

Currently, there are six states, along with Puerto Rico, which participate in the Rapid REPAT program. See Figure 4.4.

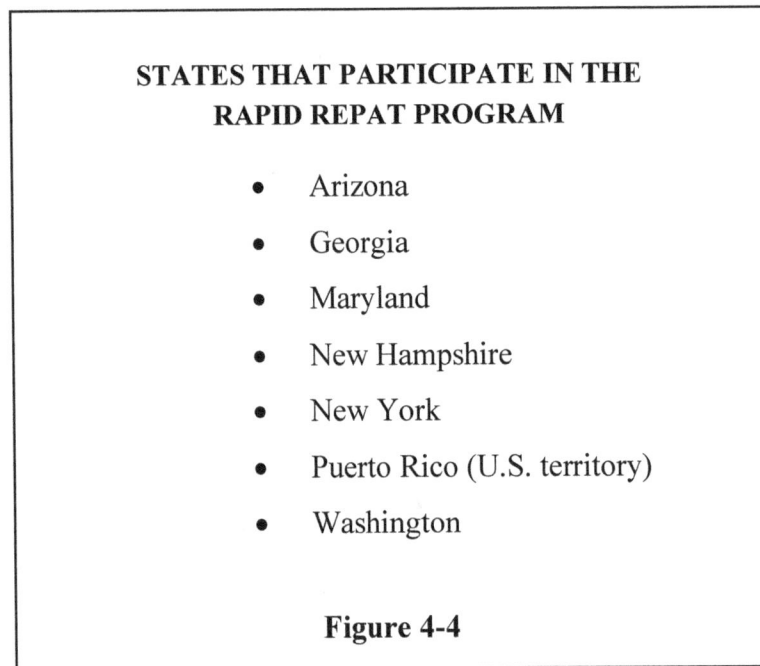

STATES THAT PARTICIPATE IN THE RAPID REPAT PROGRAM

- Arizona
- Georgia
- Maryland
- New Hampshire
- New York
- Puerto Rico (U.S. territory)
- Washington

Figure 4-4

As part of this joint partnership, a Memorandum of Agreement (MOA) or Memorandum of Understanding (MOU) is developed between ICE and the state agency—usually the Department of Corrections. An example copy of the Memorandum of Understanding between ICE and the state of New Hampshire's Department of Corrections can be found in Appendix E of this book. Under these partnerships, state agencies agree to contact ICE and provide it with biographical data about any non-U.S. citizen prisoners who enter its correctional system. This allows ICE to run a check on these prisoners to see if any of them are in the country illegally and if so, to begin the removal process. When a final order of removal is obtained for any state prisoner, ICE forwards the order to the state agency (along with a request that an immigration detainer be placed on that prisoner). At that point, the state agency does a review of the person's file to determine if he or she meets the eligibility requirements for inclusion in the Rapid REPAT program. If the state agency determines that the non-U.S. citizen prisoner is eligible, it contacts the prisoner, explains the program to the prisoner, and determines whether the prisoner wishes to voluntarily participate in the program. If the prisoner wishes to do so, he or she is asked to sign a consent form. See Appendix F, which explains the procedures for the state of New Hampshire.

The example consent form (Figure 4-5), which is based on the actual consent form used by the New Hampshire Department of Corrections, shows that a state prisoner must acknowledge that: (1) a final deportation order has been issued against the prisoner; (2) if he or she cooperates with the deportation process, he or she will be transferred to the custody of ICE; (3) ICE will make every effort to secure travel documentation so that the person can be returned to his or her home country; (4) if ICE is unable to effect the person's deportation, through no fault of the prisoner, he or she will be returned to state custody; (5) if the person is terminated from the Rapid REPAT program due to the person's actions, he or she will be returned to state custody to complete his or her sentence and may be held financially responsible for any expense associated with the person's return to state custody; (6) the person has been provided with written notice with regards to the penalties should the person illegally return to the United States; (7) he or she is voluntarily participating in the Rapid REPAT program; and (8) he or she waives any extradition challenges to his or her return to state custody to complete the remainder of his or her sentence should the prisoner illegally return to the United States.

As you can see, under the Rapid REPEAT program, a state prisoner only participates in the final stage of the state procedure (signing of the consent form)—and only after state officials have contacted the prisoner.

Rapid REPAT Offender Consent Form

I _____hereby consent and express my willingness
(Offender's Name)

to participate in the **REPAT** (Removal of Eligible Parolees Accepted for Transfer)
program, as evidenced by my initials after each provision, and my signature below.

1. I understand that a final order of deportation has been issued against me by the
   immigration judge or other qualified entity. _____

2. With my continued cooperation, I will be transferred to the custody of ICE. _____

3. ICE will endeavor to secure travel documentation, which will permit my deportation
   to my country of citizenship. _____

4. If, through no fault of my own, ICE is unable to effect my deportation, I will be
   returned to the NH Department of Corrections (NHDOC) at the State's expense to
   continue with my incarceration. _____

5. If I am terminated from the Rapid REPAT due to my own lack of cooperation, I
   understand that I will be returned to the NHDOC to continue with my incarceration
   and I may be held financially responsible for some or all of the expenses incurred in
   effecting my return to the NHDOC. _____

6. I have been provided with written notice that reentry into the United States after
   deportation constitutes a Federal, criminal offense. _____

7. I agree to participate in Rapid REPAT knowingly and voluntarily. No other promises,
   rewards, inducements or threats have been made to me in exchange for my
   cooperation. _____

8. I waive any and all rights of extradition which would challenge my return to the
   NHDOC to complete the remainder of my sentence.

_____   _____
Offender's signature   Date

_____   _____
Witness   Date

Figure 4-5

However, that does not mean that if you believe you are eligible for immigration early release you should sit back and wait for state officials to contact you. Rather, you should independently ascertain whether you are eligible for the Rapid REPAT program. And if so, you should contact your state's department of corrections staff to ensure that your biographical data has been forwarded to ICE so that the agency can begin the process of obtaining a final order of deportation.

The second category involves those states that do not participate in the Rapid REPAT program but nevertheless offer different types of immigration early release to alien prisoners. One type of early release is similar to the Rapid REPAT program in that once the person has completed a certain portion of his or her sentence, he or she can apply for early release. Under Connecticut General Statute § 54-125d, for example, if a non-U.S. citizen prisoner has completed 50% of his or her sentence, that prisoner may apply for immigration early release. Another type allows a parole eligible state prisoner to "informally" request release to ICE custody. Still another type of early release allows a defendant to negotiate in his or her plea agreement early release to ICE custody. This last type is done mainly in the state of Wyoming, but does not preclude defendants from other states (or federal defendants) from negotiating similar deals. This category is more thoroughly discussed in the next chapter.

APPENDIX D
(RAPID REPAT FACT SHEET)

Fact Sheet: Rapid REPAT

U.S. Immigration and Customs Enforcement (ICE) identifies and removes criminal aliens from the United States. The ICE Rapid REPAT (Removal of Eligible Parolees Accepted for Transfer) program is designed to expedite that process by allowing select criminal aliens incarcerated in state prisons to accept early release in exchange for voluntarily returning to their country of origin.

Background

In November 2007, ICE began meeting with state executive agencies to discuss the concept of ICE Rapid REPAT as part of the ICE ACCESS (Agreements of Cooperation in Communities to Enhance Safety and Security) initiative. The concept, implemented in Georgia and Rhode Island, is modeled after two programs in the states of New York and Arizona that capitalize on ICE's ability to more effectively identify and ultimately remove criminal aliens from the United States while still preserving the integrity of the criminal justice system. There are seven states currently participating in ICE Rapid REPAT: Arizona, Georgia, Maryland, New Hampshire, New York, Puerto Rico and Washington. ICE field offices continue to reach out to state agencies to present ICE ACCESS partnership opportunities, including ICE Rapid REPAT.

Benefits

The ICE Rapid REPAT program allows ICE to more effectively achieve its objective of identifying and quickly removing criminal aliens from the United States. The identification and processing of incarcerated criminal aliens prior to release reduces the burden on the taxpayer and ensures that criminal aliens are promptly removed from the United States upon completion of their criminal sentence. ICE Rapid REPAT also allows ICE and participating states to reduce the costs associated with detention space. The seven participating states have realized substantial savings in detention and related operating costs through ICE Rapid REPAT because prisoners are detained for significantly less time. Since the inception of ICE Rapid REPAT, the participating states have realized more than $477 million in combined cost savings.

Key Elements

Prior to implementing the Rapid REPAT program, ICE and the participating state must enter into a Memorandum of Agreement (MOA) and develop a Standard Operating Procedure (SOP). Eligible prisoners volunteer to participate in ICE Rapid REPAT and agree to waive administrative and judicial rights as a condition of their early release and removal from the United States.

Eligibility Criteria

- Criminal alien is at least 18 years of age;

- Criminal alien is not a native or citizen of the United States;

- Criminal alien voluntarily consents and agrees to participate in ICE Rapid REPAT;

- Criminal alien is imprisoned pursuant to a final conviction for an eligible nonviolent offense;

- Participating state certifies that removal of the criminal alien is appropriate and in the best interest of the state;

- Criminal alien has exhausted, or has freely and voluntarily waived, all administrative and judicial appellate rights to contest the alien's criminal conviction;

- Criminal alien agrees in writing to fully cooperate in obtaining a travel document; and

- Criminal alien has been advised that re-entry into the United States requires his/her return to participating state's custody to serve the remainder of the sentence and that s/he may be subject to prosecution pursuant to section 276 of the INA, 8 U.S.C. § 1326, including enhanced penalties.

APPENDIX E
(EXAMPLE OF MEMORANDUM OF UNDERSTANDING)

The Early Release Provision / David Mathis

MEMORANDUM OF UNDERSTANDING
BETWEEN
UNITED STATES IMMIGRATION AND CUSTOMS ENFORCEMENT, OFFICE OF DETENTION AND REMOVAL OPERATIONS, AND THE STATE OF NEW HAMPSHIRE REGARDING
THE RAPID REPATRIATION OF REMOVABLE CUSTODIAL ALIENS FROM THE UNITED STATES TO THEIR HOME COUNTRIES

I. PARTIES.

The parties to this Memorandum of Understanding (MOU) are U.S. Immigration and Customs Enforcement (ICE), as represented by the Office of Detention and Removal Operations (DRO), and the New Hampshire Department of Corrections (NHDOC).

II. AUTHORITY.

Section 241(a)(4)(B)(ii) of the Immigration and Nationality Act (INA or Act), codified at 8 U.S.C. § 1231(a)(4)(B)(ii), as amended by the Homeland Security Act of 2002, Pub. L. No. 107-296, 116 Stat. 2135 (2002), authorizes the Secretary of the Department of Homeland Security, acting through the Assistant Secretary of ICE, in coordination with a State or political subdivision of a State, to remove certain aliens in the custody of that State prior to completion of a sentence of imprisonment. New Hampshire Revised Statute § 651:25, VII (2009) authorizes the Commissioner of Corrections to release a removal prisoner to the custody of ICE. This MOU constitutes a written agreement as to the exercise of these authorities.

III. PURPOSE.

The purpose of this MOU is to set forth terms by which ICE and NHDOC will cooperate in a Rapid Repatriation of Eligible Custodial Aliens Accepted for Transfer (Rapid REPAT) program, which allows the State of New Hampshire to release a prisoner who is serving a New Hampshire state sentence to the custody of ICE, and allows ICE to remove certain aliens in the custody of a State prior to completion of a sentence of imprisonment.

IV. RESPONSIBILITIES:

A. NHDOC undertakes the following responsibilities:

1) NHDOC will initiate the Rapid REPAT process by identifying eligible custodial aliens confined pursuant to a final conviction for a nonviolent offense as defined in section 241(a)(4)(B)(i) of the INA, 8 U.S.C. § 1231(a)(4)(B)(i), and determining that the removal is appropriate and in the best interest of the State of New Hampshire. In addition, NHDOC will determine whether a prisoner may be released pursuant to New Hampshire Revised Statute § 651:25, VII (2009), whereby the prisoner must have served at least 1/3 of the minimum sentence imposed by the court; the prisoner was not convicted of a violent crime, or any crime of obstruction of justice, or sentenced to an extended term of imprisonment under New Hampshire Revised Statute § 651:6; and the prisoner was not convicted of a sexual offense as defined in New Hampshire Revised Statute § 651-B:1, V. NHDOC must submit a written request to ICE for removal of such aliens as required

77

pursuant to section 241(a)(4)(B)(ii) of the INA, 8 U.S.C. § 1231(a)(4)(B)(ii). A final conviction is a judgment of conviction as to which all rights of direct appellate review have been exhausted or waived.

2) NHDOC will only identify a custodial alien as eligible for Rapid REPAT if the alien has exhausted, or has freely and voluntarily waived in writing, all administrative and judicial appellate rights to the removal order, and if the alien agrees in writing to fully cooperate with ICE to obtain valid travel documentation and otherwise facilitate removal. *See* INA § 243(a)(1), 8 U.S.C. § 1253(a)(1). Upon an eligible alien's election to participate in Rapid REPAT, NHDOC will provide ICE with documentation evidencing the alien's waiver and agreement to cooperate with ICE to obtain valid travel documentation and to otherwise facilitate with the removal, and such documentation must be signed by the alien.

3) Once ICE accepts an alien into the Rapid REPAT program, receives appropriate documentation evidencing the alien's waiver and agreement, and determines that the alien's removal is significantly likely in the reasonably foreseeable future, NHDOC will coordinate with ICE to schedule a conditional release date for the alien to be transferred to ICE. Aliens who do not require a law enforcement escort and who possess valid travel documents can be scheduled in advance for removal so that when ICE takes custody of the alien, the alien can be removed within seventy-two (72) hours.

4) In the event of a disqualifying condition, NHDOC will promptly return the alien to State custody to finish out the remainder of his/her sentence. Disqualifying conditions include but are not limited to cases where: a valid travel document cannot be obtained for the alien within thirty (30) days of the alien entering into ICE custody; the alien seeks administrative or judicial review or challenges his or her removal order, conviction or sentence; ICE determines that removal is not significantly likely in the reasonably foreseeable future; or ICE determines that the alien otherwise failed to cooperate with ICE. NHDOC must take custody of the alien and transport the alien, at its own expense, within seventy-two (72) hours of being so notified by ICE as to any disqualifying condition. NHDOC will maintain exclusive control and responsibility for the custody and transportation of aliens from any ICE detention facility to any NHDOC prison facility in the event of notice by ICE of a disqualifying condition.

5) NHDOC will provide written notice, as required under section 241(a)(4)(C) of the INA, 8 U.S.C. § 1231(a)(4)(C), to aliens identified as eligible for Rapid REPAT of the penalties under the law of the United States relating to the reentry of deported aliens, including re-entry into the United States requires return of such aliens to NHDOC to finish out the remainder of their sentences and that such aliens are also subject to prosecution pursuant to section 276 of the INA, 8 U.S.C. § 1326, whereby expanded penalties for aliens removed under this program exists. The alien must waive in writing any and all rights of extradition which would challenge the alien's return to NHDOC to complete the remainder of his/her sentence. NHDOC must obtain acknowledgment in writing that these notices were given to aliens identified as eligible for Rapid REPAT.

The Early Release Provision / David Mathis

6) NHDOC shall arrange for the alien's transportation back to New Hampshire at state expense to complete the remainder of his/her sentence within seventy-two (72) hours of ICE's notification that the alien has reentered the United States. NHDOC will maintain exclusive control and responsibility for the custody and transportation of an alien from any ICE detention facility to any NHDOC prison facility.

B. ICE undertakes the following responsibilities:

1) When NHDOC identifies a custodial alien as eligible for Rapid REPAT pursuant to section IV.A.1 of this MOU, ICE will evaluate the alien's administrative file and relevant databases to ascertain if there is an administratively final order of removal. If no final order exists, ICE will notify NHDOC that the alien is not currently eligible for Rapid REPAT. If the alien is subject to a final order, ICE will then determine if removal of the alien is significantly likely in the reasonably foreseeable future. If the alien's removal is not reasonably foreseeable, ICE will notify NHDOC that it will not take custody of the alien because the alien's removal from the United States is not significantly likely in the reasonably foreseeable future. If ICE determines that the alien can be removed in the reasonably foreseeable future, ICE will notify NHDOC that the alien has been tentatively accepted into the Rapid REPAT program. ICE reserves the right of refusal to accept any alien into the program.

2) ICE will assume custody of an alien for Rapid REPAT purposes only if, the custodial alien has exhausted or waived all administrative and judicial appellate rights, including any collateral rights to contest the alien's removal order. However, in the event of a disqualifying condition as defined in paragraph IV.A.4, ICE shall notify NHDOC of the disqualifying condition so that NHDOC can transport the alien back to state custody at NHDOC expense, within 72 hours of notification.

3) Upon encountering an alien removed pursuant to this program who thereafter reenters the United States, ICE will notify NHDOC of the reentry so that NHDOC can arrange for the alien's transportation back to NHDOC custody, pursuant to paragraph IV.A.6 of this MOU, to complete his/her state sentence. As noted above, such aliens may also be subject to federal prosecution pursuant to section 276 of the INA, 8 U.S.C. § 1326.

V. POINTS OF CONTACT.

ICE and NHDOC points of contact (POC) for purposes of this MOU are identified in Appendix A. POC designations can be updated at any time by providing a revised Appendix A to the other party to this MOU.

VI. OTHER PROVISIONS.

A. Nothing in this MOU is intended to conflict with current law or regulation or the directives of DHS, ICE or NHDOC. If a term of this MOU is inconsistent with such authority, then that particular term shall be invalid, but the remaining terms and conditions of this agreement shall remain in full force and effect.

B. This MOU shall not be construed to affect the existing procedure with regard to the identification of, and notification to ICE of alien inmates in the custody of the NHDOC who do not qualify for the Rapid REPAT program under this MOU and who are or may be subject to removal from the United States upon their release from incarceration.

C. This MOU is an internal arrangement between ICE and NHDOC and does not create or confer any right or benefit on any other person or party, private or public.

D. Each Party is responsible for any expenses it incurs as a result of activities under this MOU. Notwithstanding any language contained herein, nothing in this MOU is meant to imply that Congress or the State of New Hampshire will appropriate funds to conduct activities provided for under this MOU.

E. Each Party is responsible for liability incurred by its own employees as a result of activities undertaken pursuant to the terms of this MOU. In the event either party is sued based in any part on activities undertaken pursuant to this MOU, such party is to notify the other party of the initiation of the suit as soon as practicable, but in any event, not later than 14 days after the party has notice of the filing of the lawsuit.

F. Both parties may, at their discretion, communicate the substance of this MOU to organizations and groups expressing an interest in the law enforcement activities to be engaged in under this MOU. It is the practice of ICE to provide a copy of this MOU to requesting media outlets only after it has been signed; the NHDOC is authorized to do the same. The NHDOC hereby agrees to coordinate with ICE prior to releasing any information relating to, or exchanged under, this MOU, including any standard operating procedures developed for the implementation of this MOU. Information obtained or developed as a result of this MOU is under the control of ICE and shall be subject to public disclosure only pursuant to the provisions of applicable federal laws, regulations, and executive orders. The State of New Hampshire hereby agrees to coordinate with ICE prior to releasing any information relating to, or exchanged under, this MOU, including any standard operating procedures developed for the implementation of this MOU. Insofar as any documents created by the NHDOC contain information developed or obtained as a result of this MOU, such documents shall not be considered public records. The release of statistical information regarding the Rapid REPAT program must be coordinated with the ICE Office of Public Affairs. The NHDOC hereby agrees to coordinate with ICE regarding information to be released to the media regarding actions taken under this MOU. The points of contact for ICE and the NHDOC for this purpose are identified in Appendix B.

VII. EFFECTIVE DATE.

The terms of this MOU will become effective on the date on which the last of the below parties signs the MOU.

The Early Release Provision / David Mathis

Attachment 1
Page 5 of 7

VIII. MODIFICATION.
Modifications to this MOA must be proposed in writing and approved and signed by the signatories.

IX. TERMINATION.
The terms of this MOU, will remain in effect from the date of signing until it is terminated by either party. Either party, upon written notice to the other party, may terminate the MOU at any time. A termination notice shall be delivered personally or by certified or registered mail and termination shall take effect immediately upon receipt of such notice.

Either party, upon written or oral notice to the other party, may temporarily suspend activities under this MOU when resource constraints or competing priorities necessitate. Notice of termination or suspension by either party shall be given to the POC named in Appendix A.

By signing this MOU, each party represents it is fully authorized to enter into this MOU, accepts the terms, responsibilities, obligations, and limitations of this MOU, and agrees to be bound thereto to the fullest extent allowed by law.

APPROVED BY:

_____
Field Office Director Dorothy Herrera-Niles
ICE, Detention and Removal Operations

_____
Commissioner William Wrenn
New Hampshire Department of Corrections

Date: _____

Date: _____

81

APPENDIX F
(NEW HAMPSHIRE DEPARTMENT OF CORRECTIONS RAPID REPAT POLICY AND PROCEDURE)

NH DEPARTMENT OF CORRECTIONS POLICY AND PROCEDURE DIRECTIVE		CHAPTER General Administration	
		STATEMENT NUMBER 5.21	
SUBJECT: **RAPID REPATRIATION OF DEPORTABLE OFFENDERS**		EFFECTIVE DATE	04/18/14
		REVIEW DATE	04/18/15
PROPONENT: William Wrenn, Commissioner		SUPERSEDES PPD#	5.21
Name/Title			
Commissioner's Office 271-5606		DATED	04/18/13
Title *Phone #*			
ISSUING OFFICER:		DIRECTOR'S INITIALS	
		DATE	
William Wrenn, Commissioner		APPENDIX ATTACHED:	
		YES NO	
REFERENCE NO: See reference section on last page of PPD.			

I.   PURPOSE:
To establish policy and procedures for the identification and release of certain aliens in the custody of the New Hampshire Department of Corrections (NHDOC) serving a state sentence, to the custody of U.S. Immigration and Customs Enforcement (ICE) prior to the completion of their state sentence.

II.   APPLICABILITY:
To all staff

III.   POLICY:
It is the policy of the NHDOC to establish an MOU (see Attachment 1) with ICE under the Rapid Repatriation of Eligible Custodial Aliens Accepted for Transfer (Rapid REPAT) program which allows the NHDOC to release an alien prisoner serving a state sentence to the custody of ICE and allows ICE to remove certain aliens prior to the completion of their sentence for the purpose of deportation.

IV.   PROCEDURE:
1.   NH State Prison Reception and Diagnostics Unit and the NH State Prison for Women will forward their intake sheets to ICE on a daily basis. These intakes sheets will be forwarded to the ICE contact noted on Appendix A of Attachment 1.
2.   NHDOC will generate and forward an inmate roster to ICE on a monthly basis. This roster will be forwarded to the ICE contact for implementation of the MOU noted on Appendix A of Attachment 1.
3.   After review of the aforementioned documents ICE will notify NHDOC of their intention regarding certain aliens who may be deportable. This intention (Detainer) will be entered into CORIS and implementation of the Rapid REPAT will begin.
4.   The NHDOC will initiate the Rapid REPAT process by identifying eligible custodial aliens confined pursuant to a final conviction for a non-violent offense as defined in the MOU, and determining that the removal is appropriate and in the best interest of the State of New

Hampshire. A final conviction is a judgment of conviction as to which all rights of direct appellate review have been exhausted or waived.

5. The NHDOC will determine whether an alien prisoner-may be released pursuant to NH RSA 651:25, VII (as inserted by Chapter 144:63 of HB 2, 2009)) (see Attachment 2), whereby the alien prisoner must have served at least 1/3 of the minimum sentence imposed by the court; the alien prisoner was not convicted of a violent crime, or any crime of obstruction of justice, or sentenced to an extended term of imprisonment under NH RSA 651:6 (see Attachment 3); and the alien prisoner was not convicted of a sexual offense as defined in NH RSA 651-B:1, V (see Attachment 4)

6. The NHDOC will only identify a custodial alien as eligible for Rapid REPAT if the alien has exhausted, or has freely and voluntarily waived in writing, all administrative and judicial appellate rights to the removal order, and if the alien agrees in writing to fully cooperate with ICE to obtain valid travel documentation and otherwise facilitate removal (see MOU). Upon an eligible alien's election to participate in Rapid REPAT, NHDOC will provide ICE with documentation evidencing the alien's waiver and agreement to cooperate with ICE to obtain valid travel documentation and to otherwise facilitate with the removal; such documentation must be signed by the alien.

7. The NHDOC will submit a written request (Attachment 6) to ICE for removal of such aliens as required pursuant to the MOU.

8. Once ICE accepts an alien into the Rapid REPAT program, receives appropriate documentation evidencing the alien's waiver and agreement, and determines that the alien's removal is significantly likely in the reasonably foreseeable future, NHDOC will coordinate with ICE to schedule a conditional release date for the alien to be transferred to ICE. Aliens who do not require a law enforcement escort and who possess valid travel documents can be scheduled in advance for removal so that when ICE takes custody of the alien, the alien can be removed within 72 hours.

9. In the event of a disqualifying condition, NHDOC will promptly return the alien to State custody to finish out the remainder of his/her sentence. Disqualifying conditions include but are not limited to cases where: valid travel documents cannot be obtained for the alien within 30 days of the alien entering into ICE custody; the alien seeks administrative or judicial review or challenges his or her removal order, conviction or sentence; ICE determines that removal is not significantly likely in the reasonably foreseeable future; or ICE determines that the alien otherwise failed to cooperate with ICE. NHDOC must take custody of the alien and transport the alien, at its own expense, within 72 hours of being so notified by ICE as to any disqualifying condition. NHDOC will maintain exclusive control and responsibility for the custody and transportation of aliens from any ICE detention facility to any NHDOC prison facility in the event of notice by ICE of a disqualifying condition.

10. NHDOC will provide written notice, as required in the MOU, to aliens identified as eligible for Rapid REPAT of the penalties under the law of the United States relating to the reentry of deported aliens, including reentry into the United States requires return of such aliens to NHDOC to finish out the remainder of their sentences and that such aliens are also subject to prosecution pursuant to section 276 of the INA, 8 U.S.C. § 1326, whereby expanded penalties for aliens removed under this program exist The alien must waive in writing any and all rights of extradition which would challenge the alien's return to NHDOC to complete the remainder of his/her sentence. NHDOC must obtain acknowledgment in writing (Attachment 6) that these notices were given to aliens identified as eligible for Rapid REPAT.

11. An alien who is rejected for the REPAT program for any reason will be returned to New Hampshire within 72 hours. The NHDOC shall arrange for the alien's transportation back to New Hampshire at state expense to complete the remainder of his/her sentence.

The Early Release Provision / David Mathis

Rapid REPAT Offender Consent Form

I _____ hereby consent and express my
(Offender's Name)

willingness to participate in the **REPAT** (Removal of Eligible Parolees Accepted for Transfer) program, as evidenced by my initials after each provision, and my signature below.

1. I understand that a final order of deportation has been issued against me by the immigration judge or other qualified entity. _____

2. With my continued cooperation, I will be transferred to the custody of ICE. _____

3. ICE will endeavor to secure travel documentation, which will permit my deportation to my country of citizenship. _____

4. If, through no fault of my own, ICE is unable to effect my deportation, I will be returned to the NH Department of Corrections (NHDOC) at the State's expense to continue with my incarceration. _____

5. If I am terminated from the Rapid REPAT due to my own lack of cooperation, I understand that I will be returned to the NHDOC to continue with my incarceration and I may be held financially responsible for some or all of the expenses incurred in effecting my return to the NHDOC. _____

6. I have been provided with written notice that reentry into the United States after deportation constitutes a Federal, criminal offense. _____

7. I agree to participate in Rapid REPAT knowingly and voluntarily. No other promises, rewards, inducements or threats have been made to me in exchange for my cooperation.
_____

8. I waive any and all rights of extradition which would challenge my return to the NHDOC to complete the remainder of my sentence.

_____   _____
Offender's signature   Date

_____   _____
Witness   Date

85

Attachment 6

Request for Rapid REPAT

Pursuant to the Memorandum of Understanding between Immigration and Customs Enforcement (ICE) and the New Hampshire Department of Corrections (NHDOC), the NHDOC requests that the offender (s) named below be accepted by ICE into the Rapid REPAT program.

Offender(s)' name(s) and date(s) of birth filled in here

Submitted on behalf of the NHDOC by:

APPENDIX G
(NEW HAMPSHIRE CRIMINAL CODES)

TITLE LXII
CRIMINAL CODE
CHAPTER 651
SENTENCES
General Provisions
Section 651:6

651:6 Extended Term of Imprisonment. –

I. A convicted person may be sentenced according to paragraph III if the jury also finds beyond a reasonable doubt that such person:

(a) Based on the circumstances for which he or she is to be sentenced, has knowingly devoted himself or herself to criminal activity as a major source of livelihood;

(b) Has been subjected to a court-ordered psychiatric examination on the basis of which the jury finds that such person is a serious danger to others due to a gravely abnormal mental condition;

(c) Has manifested exceptional cruelty or depravity in inflicting death or serious bodily injury on the victim of the crime;

(d) Has committed an offense involving the use of force against a person with the intention of taking advantage of the victim's age or physical disability;

(e) Has committed or attempted to commit any of the crimes defined in RSA 631 or 632-A against a person under 13 years of age;

(f) Was substantially motivated to commit the crime because of hostility towards the victim's religion, race, creed, sexual orientation as defined in RSA 21:49, national origin or sex;

(g) Has knowingly committed or attempted to commit any of the crimes defined in RSA 631 where he or she knows the victim was, at the time of the commission of the crime, a law enforcement officer, a paid firefighter, volunteer firefighter, on-call firefighter, or licensed emergency medical care provider as defined in RSA 153-A:2, V acting in the line of duty;

(h) Was an on-duty law enforcement officer at the time that he or she committed or attempted to commit any of the crimes defined in RSA 631;

(i) Has committed a crime listed in RSA 193-D:1 in a safe school zone under RSA 193-D;

(j) Possesses a radio device with the intent to use that device in the commission of robbery, burglary, theft, gambling, stalking, or a violation of any provision of RSA 318-B. In this section, the term ""radio device" means any device capable of receiving a wireless transmission on any frequency allocated for law enforcement use, or any device capable of transmitting and receiving a wireless transmission;

(k) Has committed or attempted to commit negligent homicide as defined in RSA 630:3, I against a person under 13 years of age who was in the care of, or under the supervision of, the defendant at the time of the offense;

(l) Has committed or attempted to commit any of the crimes defined in RSA 637 or RSA 638 against a victim who is 65 years of age or older or who has a physical or mental disability and that in perpetrating the crime, the defendant intended to take advantage of the victim's age or a physical or mental condition that impaired the victim's ability to manage his or her property or financial resources or to protect his or her rights or interests;

(m) Has committed or attempted to commit aggravated felonious sexual assault in violation of RSA 632-A:2, I(l) or RSA 632-A:2, II where the defendant was 18 years of age or older at the time of the offense;

(n) Has committed or attempted to commit aggravated felonious sexual assault in violation of RSA 632-A:2, III, and one or more of the acts comprising the pattern of sexual assault was an offense under RSA 632-A:2, I(l) or RSA 632-A:2, II, or both, and the defendant was 18 years of age or older when the pattern of sexual assault began;

[Paragraph I(o) effective until March 31, 2009; see also paragraph I(o) set out below.]

(o) Has purposely, knowingly, or recklessly with extreme indifference to the value of human life committed an act or acts constituting first degree assault as defined in RSA 631:1 against a person under 13 years of age where the serious bodily injury has resulted in brain damage or physical disability to the child that is likely to be permanent; or

[Paragraph I(o) effective March 31, 2009; see also paragraph I(o) set out above.]

(o) Has purposely, knowingly, or recklessly with extreme indifference to the value of human life committed an act or acts constituting first degree assault as defined in RSA 631:1 against a person under 13 years of age where the serious bodily injury has resulted in brain damage or physical disability to the child that is likely to be permanent;

[Paragraph I(p) effective until March 31, 2009; see also paragraph I(p) set out below.]

(p) Has committed murder as defined in RSA 630:1-b against a person under 13 years of age.

[Paragraph I(p) effective March 31, 2009; see also paragraph I(p) set out above.]

(p) Has committed murder as defined in RSA 630:1-b against a person under 13 years of age; or

[Paragraph I(q) effective March 31, 2009.]

(q) Has knowingly committed any of the following offenses as a criminal street gang member, or for the benefit of, at the direction of, or in association with any criminal street gang, with the purpose to promote, further, or assist in any such criminal conduct by criminal street gang members:

(1) Violent crime as defined in RSA 651:5, XIII.

(2) A crime involving the distribution, sale, or manufacture of a controlled drug under RSA 318-B:2.

(3) Class A felony theft where the property stolen was a firearm.

(4) Unlawful sale of a pistol or a revolver.

(5) Witness tampering.

(6) Criminal street gang solicitation as defined in RSA 644:20.

[Paragraph I-a effective until March 31, 2009; see also paragraph I-a set out below.]

I-a. As used in this section, a ""law enforcement officer" is a sheriff or deputy sheriff of any county, a state police officer, a constable or police officer of any city or town, an official or employee of any prison, jail, or corrections institution, a probation-parole officer, a juvenile probation and parole officer, or a conservation officer.

[Paragraph I-a effective March 31, 2009; see also paragraph I-a set out above.]

I-a. As used in this section:

(a) ""Law enforcement officer" means a sheriff or deputy sheriff of any county, a state police officer, a constable or police officer of any city or town, an official or employee of any prison, jail, or corrections institution, a probation-parole officer, a juvenile probation and parole officer, or a conservation officer.

(b) ""Criminal street gang member" means an individual to whom 2 or more of the following apply:

(1) Admits to criminal street gang membership;

(2) Is identified as a criminal street gang member by a law enforcement officer, parent, guardian, or documented reliable informant;

(3) Resides in or frequents a particular criminal street gang's area and adopts its style of dress, its use of hand or other signs, tattoos, or other physical markings, and associates with known criminal street gang members; or

(4) Has been arrested more than once in the company of individuals who are identified as criminal street gang members by law enforcement, for offenses that are consistent with usual criminal street gang activity.

(c) ""Criminal street gang" means a formal or informal ongoing organization, association, or group of 3 or more persons, which has as one of its primary objectives or activities the commission of criminal activity, whose members share a common name, identifying sign, symbol, physical marking, style of dress, or use of hand sign, and whose members individually or collectively have engaged in the commission, attempted commission, solicitation to commit, or conspiracy to commit 2 or more the following offenses, or a reasonably equivalent offense in another jurisdiction, on separate occasions within the preceding 3 years:

(1) Violent crimes, as defined in RSA 651:5, XIII;

(2) Distribution, sale, or manufacture of a controlled drug in violation of RSA 318-B:2;

(3) Class A felony theft;

(4) Unlawful sale of a pistol or revolver; or

(5) Witness tampering.

II. A convicted person may be sentenced according to the terms of paragraph III if the court finds, and includes such findings in the record, that such person:

(a) Has twice previously been convicted in this state, or in another jurisdiction, on sentences in excess of one year;

(b) Has previously been convicted of a violation of RSA 630:3, II, RSA 265-A:3, I(b) or II(b), or any crime in any other jurisdiction involving driving or attempting to drive a motor vehicle under the influence of controlled drugs or intoxicating liquors, or both, and such person has committed a crime as defined under RSA 630:3, II or RSA 265-A:3, I(b) or II(b); or

(c) Has twice previously been convicted in this state or any other jurisdiction, for driving or attempting to drive a motor vehicle under the influence of intoxicating liquors or controlled drugs, or both, and such person has committed a crime as defined under RSA 630:3, II or RSA

265-A:3, I(b) or II(b).

III. If authorized by paragraph I or II, and if written notice of the possible application of this section is given the defendant at least 21 days prior to the commencement of jury selection for his or her trial, a defendant may be sentenced to an extended term of imprisonment. An extended term is, for a person convicted of:

(a) Any felony, other than murder or manslaughter, a minimum to be fixed by the court of not more than 10 years and a maximum to be fixed by the court of not more than 30 years;

(b) A misdemeanor, a minimum to be fixed by the court of not more than 2 years and a maximum to be fixed by the court of not more than 5 years;

(c) Manslaughter, a minimum to be fixed by the court of not more than 20 years and a maximum to be fixed by the court of not more than 40 years;

(d) Murder, life imprisonment;

(e) Two or more offenses under RSA 632-A:2, life imprisonment without parole;

(f) A third offense under RSA 632-A:3, life imprisonment; or

(g) Any of the crimes listed under RSA 651:6, I(j), a minimum to be fixed by the court of not less than 90 days and a maximum of not more than one year.

IV. If authorized by subparagraphs I(m), (n), or (o) and if notice of the possible application of this section is given to the defendant prior to the commencement of trial:

(a) There is a presumption that a person shall be sentenced to a minimum to be fixed by the court of not less than 25 years and a maximum of life imprisonment unless the court makes a determination that the goals of deterrence, rehabilitation, and punishment would not be served, based on the specific circumstances of the case, by such a sentence and the court makes specific written findings in support of the lesser sentence. Before the court can determine whether the presumption has been overcome, the court shall consider, but is not limited to, the following factors:

(1) Age of victim at time of offense.

(2) Age of the defendant at the time of the offense.

(3) Relationship between defendant and victim.

(4) Injuries to victim.

(5) Use of force, fear, threats, or coercion to the victim or another.

(6) Length of time defendant offended against victim.

(7) Number of times defendant offended against victim.

(8) Number of other victims.

(9) Acceptance of responsibility by defendant.

(10) Defendant's criminal history.

(11) Use of a weapon.

(12) Medical or psychological condition of the victim at the time of the assault.

(b) The sentence shall also include, in addition to any other penalties provided by law, a special sentence of lifetime supervision by the department of corrections. The defendant shall comply with the conditions of lifetime supervision which are imposed by the court or the department of corrections. Violation of any of the conditions of lifetime supervision shall be deemed contempt of court. The special sentence of lifetime supervision shall begin upon the offender's release from incarceration, parole, or probation. A defendant who is sentenced to lifetime supervision pursuant to this paragraph shall not be eligible for release from the lifetime supervision pursuant to RSA 632-A:10-a, V(b).

(c) Any decision by the superior court under subparagraph (a) may be reviewed by the sentence review division of the superior court at the request of the defendant or at the request of the state pursuant to RSA 651:58.

V. If authorized by subparagraph I(p) and if notice of the possible application of this section is given to the defendant prior to the commencement of trial, a person shall be sentenced to an extended term of imprisonment as follows: a minimum to be fixed by the court of not less than 35 years and a maximum of life imprisonment.

VI. A person shall be sentenced according to the terms of paragraph VII if the court finds, and includes such findings in the record, that such person:

(a) (1) Committed a violation of RSA 632-A:2, I(l), RSA 632-A:2, II, or RSA 632-A:2, III, in which one or more of the acts comprising the pattern of sexual assault was an offense under RSA 632-A:2, I(l) or RSA 632-A:2, II, or both, after having previously been convicted of an offense in violation of one of the aforementioned offenses or any other statute prohibiting the same conduct in another state, territory or possession of the United States, and

(2) The person committed the subsequent offense while released on bail on the earlier offense or the sentence for the earlier conviction involved a term of incarceration, probation, parole, or other supervised release; or

(b) (1) Committed a violation of RSA 631:1 after having previously been convicted of an offense in violation of RSA 631:1, or any other statute prohibiting the same conduct in another state, territory or possession of the United States, if the earlier offense also involved a victim under 13 years of age where the serious bodily injury resulted in brain damage or physical disability to the child that is likely to be permanent; and

(2) The person committed the subsequent offense while released on bail on the earlier offense or the sentence for the earlier conviction involved a term of incarceration, probation, parole, or other supervised release; or

(c) (1) Committed a violation of RSA 630:1-b after having previously been convicted of an offense in violation of RSA 630:1-b, or any other statute prohibiting the same conduct in another state, territory, or possession of the United States; and

(2) The person committed the subsequent offense while released on bail on the earlier offense or the sentence for the earlier conviction involved a term of incarceration, probation, parole, or other supervised release.

VII. If the court has made the findings authorized by RSA 651:6, VI, and if notice of the possible application of this section is given to the defendant prior to the commencement of trial, a person shall be sentenced to an extended term of imprisonment of life without parole.

Source. 1971, 518:1. 1973, 370:3. 1981, 511:1. 1985, 228:7, 8. 1990, 68:1; 140:2, XI. 1992, 3:1. 1994, 355:4. 1995, 131:1, 2. 1996, 198:1. 1997, 108:16. 1998, 301:1, 2. 1999, 296:2. 2003, 33:1. 2006, 89:1, 2; 197:1; 260:357; 327:177; 327:18, 20, eff. Jan. 1, 2007 at 12:01 a.m. 2007, 110:1, eff. June 11, 2007. 2008, 379:1, 2, eff. Mar. 31, 2009.

CHAPTER 5
ADDITIONAL EARLY RELEASE PROGRAMS

———————◇•○○•◇———————

In the last chapter you learned that under federal law the U.S. Attorney General has the power to grant early release to state non-U.S. citizen prisoners who meet certain conditions. First, the state prisoner's conviction must be final, that is, he or she must be done with the appeal process. Second, returning the prisoner to his or her home country must be in the best interest of the state. Third, a written request from the governor or the governor's designated representative must be sent to the U.S. Attorney General. See Figure 5-1.

In addition, under section 1231(a)(4)(B)(ii), the state alien prisoner cannot be serving time for a violent crime or a "nonviolent" crime listed under section 1101(a)(43)(C) or 1101(a)(43)(E). See Figure 5-2. As noted in the last chapter, the crimes listed under these sections are federal crimes. Any similar type of crime committed under state law, however, may make a state prisoner ineligible for immigration early release. For instance, under §1101(a)(43)(E), it is illegal for a felon to possess explosive materials as defined by 18 U.S.C. §824(i). Likewise, it is unlawful for a felon to possess explosive materials under Colorado law. Thus, a person convicted under that Colorado law may be ineligible for immigration early release.

You also learned in the last chapter that states can and do develop their own rules and procedures. These state procedures are the basis for this chapter. As previously mentioned, some states participate in the Rapid REPAT program; a joint federal and state program which requires those states participating in the program to forward the names and other biographical data about their non-U.S. citizen prisoners to the Immigration and Customs Enforcement (ICE) agency.

Most states, however, refuse to enter into a formal agreement with ICE and its Rapid REPAT program; thereby maintaining a degree of autonomy. The procedures of these states can be divided into three groups: (1) state prisoners who reach their parole eligibility dates and who are then informally paroled to ICE's custody; (2) state prisoners who complete a specific portion of their determinate sentence and who then request transfer to ICE custody; and (3) state prisoners who negotiate immigration early release transfers in their plea agreements. (See Figure 5-3).

The State Provision
(8 U.S.C. §1231(a)(4)(B)(ii))

(a) **Detention, release, and removal of aliens ordered removed**

(4) **Aliens imprisoned, arrested, or on parole, supervised release, or probation**
(A) **In general**
Except as provided in section 259(a) of title 42 and paragraph (2) the Attorney General may not remove an alien who is sentenced to imprisonment until the alien is released from imprisonment. Parole, supervised release, probation, or possibility of arrest or further imprisonment is not a reason to defer removal.
(B) **Exception for removal of nonviolent offenders prior to completion of sentence of imprisonment**
The Attorney General is authorized to remove an alien in accordance with applicable procedures under this chapter before the alien has completed a sentence of imprisonment—
(ii) in the case of an alien in the custody of a State (or a political subdivision of a State), if the chief State official exercising authority with respect to the incarceration of the alien determines that
(I) the alien is confined pursuant to a final conviction for a nonviolent offense (other than an offense described in section 1101(a)(43)(C) or (E) of this title),
(II) the removal is appropriate and in the best interest of the State, and
(III) submits a written request to the Attorney General that such alien be so removed.

Figure 5-1

List of nonviolent crimes, under 8 U.S.C. §1101(a)(43), which make a *state* prisoner ineligible for early release:

(C) illicit trafficking in firearms or destructive devices
(E) an offense described in —

- 18 U.S.C. §842(h) or (i)(relating to explosive material offenses);

- 18 U.S.C. §844(d), (e), (f), (g), (h), or (i)(relating to explosive material offenses);

- 18 U.S.C. §922(g)(1), (2), (3), (4), or (5)(relating to felon or alien in possession of a firearm);

- 18 U.S.C. §922(j), (n), (o), (p), or (r)(relating to firearm offenses);

- 18 U.S.C. §924(b) or (h)(relating to firearm offenses); or

- 26 U.S.C. §5861 (relating to firearm offenses)

Figure 5-2

States **Not** Participating in Rapid REPAT But Offering Alternative Programs	
State/State Law	**Program Notes**
Colorado/C.R.S. 17-22.5-404.7	Inmates who have reached their parole eligibility dates, have been assessed as medium risk or below on the Colorado risk, assessment scale, and have an immigration detainer.
Connecticut/Conn. Gen. Stat §54-125d	Non-violent offenders must serve at least 50% of sentence; violent offenders must serve 85% of sentence in this state. However, under §54-125d(c), alien prisoners are eligible for deportation parole after serving at least 50% of sentence.
Illinois/Public Act 097-0698 Sec. 5-5-3(2)(A) and (B)	Upon a motion by the district attorney, the court may hold an alien's sentence in abeyance or suspend the sentence and remand the alien into ICE's custody.
Iowa/none	No official state law, but state parole program can informally release alien inmates to an immigration detainer.
Kansas/K.S.A. §22-3717(g)	Upon the successful completion of a prisoner's program statement, the Kansas Parole Board can grant parole and release alien prisoner to ICE's custody.

Kentucky/501 Kentucky Admin. Regs. 1:030	Under Kentucky Rev. Stat. 439.3401(3), violent offenders convicted of a capital offense or Class A felony or who is designated a Class B violent offender, must serve at least 85% of the sentence imposed. Those classified as non-violent offenders become eligible for parole after serving 20% of their sentence. Once on parole, prisoner can be released to ICE's custody.
Michigan/Mich. Compiled Laws 791.2346	A final order of removal must have been issued and the person must have served at least 1/2 of minimum sentence.
New Mexico/none	No official state law, but probation and parole officers can informally release alien inmates to ICE custody.
North Carolina/N.C. Gen. Stat. §148-64.1	The Post Release Supervision and Parole Commission may release non-violent offenders to ICE Custody if a final removal order has been received by the DOC and the offender has served at least half of the minimum sentence.
Ohio/Ohio Rev. Code Ann. 2967.17(A)(3)	Ohio state prisoners who are granted parole and who are 'taken in custody by ICE' are granted "administrative release."
Oklahoma/57 Okl. St. §332.7	A person must serve at least 50% of sentence. However, a person who

	commits a felony offense listed in 21 Okl. St. §13.1, must serve 85% of sentence before he or she is eligible for parole.

Figure 5-3 (a)

State/State Law	**Program Notes**
Pennsylvania/ 61 Pa. C.S. §6143	The Pennsylvania Board of Probation and Parole can grant early conditional release to parole and transfer an inmate to ICE's custody.
Texas/Texas Government Code §508.146(f)	Under §508.146(f), a non-violent alien may be released to ICE pending deportation on a date designated by the Texas Board of Pardons and Paroles if the alien would be deported to another country, is not a threat to public safety, and is unlikely to reenter the U.S. illegally.
Vermont/none	No official state law, but once alien is eligible for parole, he or she can request parole to ICE custody. See: www.doc.state.vt.us/about/parole-board/pb-manual
Wyoming/none	No official state law, but criminal defense attorney may negotiate in plea agreement to allow for early release to ICE custody.

Figure 5-3 (b)

Figure 5-3 gives an overview of those states that offer alternative procedures for immigration early release. If your state is not listed that does not mean that you cannot get immigration early release. Rather, the list simply contains states that have formal or informal agreements with ICE. Generally speaking, every non-U.S. citizen state prisoner can seek immigration early release on his or her own. For example, let say that a state defendant in Tennessee signs a plea agreement for a sentence of 10 years, to be served at 30%. This means that the defendant's release eligibility date (RED) would be 3 years. However, the Tennessee Board of Probation and Parole does not have to grant parole on that date. But, if that person is in the country illegally and there is an immigration detainer in the person's file, that person can ask the parole board to grant him parole to ICE's custody when he or she reaches the 30% release eligibility date.

1. **Parole Eligible Prisoners**

Of the sixteen states listed in Figure 5-3 which offer an alternative to the Rapid REPAT program, the majority of them parole their alien prisoners to ICE's custody after the prisoner has reached his or her parole eligibility date. These programs are nearly identical to the Rapid REPAT program. The big difference is that these states have not signed a "formal" agreement with ICE and as such, are not required to notify ICE about non-U.S. citizen prisoners in their custody. As a practical matter, most states do not contact ICE in order to obtain a final removal order for a prisoner, usually a prerequisite for deportation. Instead, ICE officials, using a computer database, determine whether individuals convicted of violating other local, state and federal laws have entered the country illegally. If so, they issue a detainer to the law enforcement authority holding the individual, asking the institution to keep custody of the prisoner for the agency or to let the agency know when the prisoner is about to be released.

Connecticut is one of those states that parole their prisoners to the custody of ICE. The procedure is remarkably similar to the Rapid REPAT program that you learned about in the last chapter. Indeed, the only difference is that Connecticut has not entered into a formal contract, either a Memorandum of Understanding (MOU) or Memorandum of Agreement (MOA), with ICE. However, Connecticut law specifically states that "[t]he Board of Pardons and Paroles shall enter into an agreement with the United States Immigration and Naturalization Service for the deportation of parolees who are aliens . . . and for whom an order of deportation has been issued." See Appendix H. Based on this law, Connecticut has entered into an "informal" agreement with ICE, which allows both parties to change the terms of the agreement, if and when necessary, without having to re-write a contract each time a change is made. This allows states like Connecticut to quickly and efficiently adjust their programs to match public policy or sentiment.

Under Connecticut's procedure, the Department of Corrections determines which prisoners to refer to the Board of Pardons and Paroles for an intake interview and determination of immigration status. Any non-U.S. citizen prisoner who has not been convicted of either a capital felony or a class A felony may be referred to the Board by the DOC and/or the sentencing court. One of the key features of Connecticut's program is that it allows non-U.S. citizen prisoners who have committed a violent crime to be granted parole before U.S. citizens who commit similar violent crimes. Pursuant to Connecticut General Statute §54-125a(b)(2), state prisoners who have been convicted of an offense involving the "use of force against another," i.e., a crime of violence, are ineligible for parole until he or she has served at least 85% of his or her sentence. However, under §54-125(c), a non-U.S. citizen prisoner is eligible for "deportation parole" after serving at least

50% of his or her sentence. In layman terms, this translates into a violent U.S. citizen offender serving 8½ year on a 10-year sentence while a violent non-U.S. citizen offender will serve only 5 year before being deported.

Colorado is another of those states that parole their prisoners to ICE's custody. In order for the prisoner to be eligible, however, he or she must meet several criteria. First, the prisoner must be scored as a medium risk or below to re-offend as assessed by Colorado's risk assessment scale. Second, the person cannot be serving a sentence for one of several enumerated crimes, to include but not limited to false imprisonment, internet luring of a child, unlawful possession of a firearm or incendiary device, racketeering, and use of a deadly weapon. Third, an active immigration *detainer* from ICE must have been lodged against the prisoner.[3] See Appendix I.

If the prisoner meets the above criteria and has reached his or her parole eligibility date, the Colorado Board of Parole will contact ICE so that the board of parole may release the prisoner to the custody of ICE. Once ICE issues a *final order of removal*, the Colorado Department of Corrections will request that the parole board discharge the parole—ending the prisoner's commitment to the state of Colorado.[4]

If, on the other hand, ICE withdraws its detainer or declines to take custody of the prisoner, the parole board will hold a rescission hearing and may revoke parole. Yet, the parole board is just as likely, if not more so, to leave its parole decision unchanged; which means the prisoner will be released back into the local community

---

[3] This is a big difference from other states which require a final order of removal from ICE. In Colorado, it only requires a detainer to start the process. Much later, the person can be discharged from parole after a final order of removal has been issued.

[4] Similarly, in Ohio, a state prisoner who is taken into custody by ICE and deported may be granted "administrative release." Importantly, "[a]ny person granted an administrative release under this section may subsequently apply for a commutation of sentence for the purpose of regaining the rights and privileges forfeited by conviction."

2. **Determinate Sentences**

Some states (as well as the federal government) have abolished their parole systems and now give their prisoners fixed or determinate sentences. A determinate sentence is a sentence with a definite number of months or years that is not subject to review or alteration by a parole board or similar agency. For instance, a 5-year sentence of imprisonment is determinate because the prisoner will spend no more than 5 years in prison (minus time off for good behavior, if applicable). Generally, a determinate sentence is followed by a term of supervised release or parole supervision. When a prisoner is released from incarceration, he or she has to report to a probation officer for a set number of months or years. If a prisoner violates any conditions of his or her supervised release or parole supervision, he or she may be returned to prison.

With regards to immigration early release, months or years prior to a prisoner's projected release date, ICE contacts state prison officials and informs that department about the non-U.S. citizen prisoner in its custody. At that point, ICE officials begin the removal process in an effort to obtain a final removal order. Once the removal order is obtained, ICE sends it to state prison officials, who then place a detainer on the prisoner. Before the prisoner's release date, the prisoner is transferred to ICE's custody for return to his or her home country.

The above procedure is almost exactly like the one that the Bureau of Prisons (BOP) uses with its federal non-U.S. citizen prisoners. Under both federal and state procedures, a prisoner is released to ICE's custody at the discretion of the U.S. Attorney General (federal prisoners) or governor (state prisoners). What this means is that non-U.S. citizen prisoners can be released months or even years before their projected release date.

In Chapter 2, you learned that a federal prisoner may be granted early release by simply writing a letter to the U.S. Attorney General. There is no limitation on how early the U.S. Attorney General can release a federal prisoner. For example, the federal prisoner may have been sentenced to 60 months of imprisonment, but the Attorney General decided to grant the prisoner early release after the prisoner has served only 12 months. The process for obtaining this type of relief in various states is somewhat different, as you have learned, while the amount of time a state prisoner serves before early release is granted is usually greater, on average ⅓ to ½ of his or her sentence.

However, there are some states that do not release their alien inmates to ICE's custody until a few days before the inmate's scheduled release date. Not such a great benefit. But there is a way around this pitfall.

As thoroughly discussed in my book *Pardons and Commutations of Sentences: The Complete Guidebook to Applying for Clemency*, each state's constitution has a provision that allows the governor or a designated representative to grant pardons and commutations of sentences to those individuals who have committed crimes in that particular state.

In the context of immigration early release, the non-U.S. citizen state prisoner would seek to have his or her sentence commuted, which means that the governor or a designated representative would lessen the amount of time that a state prisoner would be required to serve in prison. By way of example, say that the state court sentenced a prisoner to a 9-year sentence, but the governor commuted it to a 5-year sentence. The person would serve 5 years in prison rather than the original 9-year sentence.

Each state has its own unique procedure for applying for a commutation of sentence. See Appendix J. But generally, a prisoner fills out a petition or application and sends it either directly to the governor's office or an agency like the Board of Pardons and Paroles (for specific details on how to apply for a commutation of sentence in your state, order a copy of *Pardons and Commutations of Sentences: The Complete Guidebook to Applying for Clemency*.)

On each commutation petition or application, the prisoner is required to give a reason why he or she should be granted a commutation of sentence. While there is a myriad of things that a prisoner can list on the petition or application, one of the things that an alien prisoner should cite is the potential disparity in sentencing for persons who commit similar crimes. Let us say, for instance, that a U.S. citizen and non-U.S. citizen are convicted of fraud and given a 5-year prison sentence. While the non-U.S. citizen prisoners must serve the full 5-year term (minus any good time credit), the U.S citizen may serve months or even years less than the full 5-year term because of halfway house placement and in some cases, additional time off because of participation in special programs. In the Introduction to this book you read about Troy, a federal prisoner who had been given a 10-year prison sentence. Troy was able to earn 1-year off his sentence due to his successful completion of a drug treatment program and 11 months of halfway house placement. If Troy had been an non-U.S. citizen prisoner, he would not have been eligible for either program. Moreover, citizen prisoners can be housed in the lowest security prisons, i.e. prison camps and work-release camps, as well as home confinement. None of these programs are available to non-U.S. citizen prisoners. In one example, a non-U.S. citizen prisoner from the Dominican Republic was sentenced to 46 months in prison. Thereafter, ICE lodged an immigration detainer against him. After he had served much of his sentence, the prisoner submitted a request seeking placement in home confinement.

When his unit team denied his request, he filed numerous administrative remedy requests. Each was denied on the grounds that all non-U.S. citizen prisoners were excluded from eligibility for early release programs. The petitioner filed a motion in the district court, challenging the decisions of these prison officials. However, the court sided with prison officials and dismissed his motion. This is exactly the type of disparity that you should bring to the governor's attention when requesting a commutation of sentence.

To recap, if you are a state prisoner, you should first determine how much time you anticipate getting off your sentence under immigration early release. If you will have to do more than 50% of your sentence, you should consider applying for a commutation of sentence.

3. Plea Agreements

The final method for obtaining immigration early release is to negotiate with the district attorney (D.A.) or prosecutor to include a provision in your plea agreement.

In any criminal case, the prosecutor has broad discretion with regards to fashioning plea agreements. The prosecutor can dismiss counts, lessen the severity of the charges, and reduce possible punishments.

As discussed earlier in this book, when federal prosecutors were swamped with illegal re-entry cases in southern California, they began offering reduced sentences to defendants in exchange for the defendants agreeing to plead guilty, foregoing their appeals, and participating in a streamlined deportation process. The procedure initiated by the prosecutors in southern California eventually morphed into the federal "fast-track" program.

On the flip side, it is a little known fact that defense attorneys can assert a lot of influence on the development of a plea agreement, particularly if the evidence against a defendant is weak.

The real factor that decides cases, however, is money. It is extremely expensive for federal and state governments to prosecute a case before a jury. Added to the expense of a trial is the cost to the government of spending years fighting appeals filed by defendants. That is the principal reason that nearly all cases, whether federal or state, result in plea agreements. It is also the reason why there is a growing trend towards including appeal waivers in plea agreements. Finally, the cost of incarceration is a multi-billion dollar drain on federal and state budgets. On average, federal and state governments spend more than $30,000 per inmate each year to house, feed, and clothe inmates.

These converging forces offer defendants golden opportunities to reduce their sentences up front, thereby eliminating the need to rely on parole boards or other agencies for early release.

Let us look at the procedures used in the state of Wyoming to get a better understanding of the benefits associated with this method. As with other states (and the Federal government), prosecutors in Wyoming meet with defense attorneys to work out the terms of any plea agreement. Remember, ICE officials actively search computer databases on a regular basis to review federal, state, and local arrest records and to determine if any arrestee is in the country illegally. And if so, the agency may issue an immigration detainer request. With that being said, it is likely that both the prosecutor and defense attorney are aware of an alien defendant's immigration status. Thus, when the plea is negotiated, a provision may be added to the terms of the plea which allows the non-U.S. citizen defendant to almost immediately fall under the custody of ICE and be deported.

Here is how one Wyoming case proceeded. A non-U.S. citizen defendant (along with others) was arrested by state law enforcement officers on six counts of delivery of a non-narcotic controlled substance. After the defendant's arrest immigration officials sent a detainer request to the Platte County Sheriff. During plea negotiations, the state prosecutor offered to dismiss four of the six counts and recommend a sentence of 4 to 6 years on each of the two remaining counts, to run concurrently. The final provision allowed INS to immediately take custody of the defendant and deport him. The defendant accepted the plea offer. The judge sentenced him to 4 to 6 years on each of the two counts; to run concurrently to each other. See Figure. 5-4. Remarkably, the defendant was deported to Mexico twenty-six days after the state court sentenced him. In a nutshell, the defendant did not spend one day in state prison. He spent a total of 69 days in the county jail while his plea deal was being negotiated. That means this defendant served only 4.72% of his minimum sentence and 3.15% of his maximum sentence.[5]

Written Judgment of the District Court for the 8th District (Wyoming)

IT IS FURTHER ORDERED that upon each count, the Defendant is placed in the care, custody and control of the Department of Corrections for physical placement at a State Penal institution for a period of not less than four (4) years nor more than six (6) years. The Defendant's prison terms shall run concurrently with each other. The Defendant is given credit upon both the minimum and maximum sentences imposed herein, for forty-three (43) days already served in connection with this matter.

IT IS FURTHER ORDERED that the Defendant is remanded to the custody of the Platte County Sheriff, for incarceration in the Platte County Jail until he is transported to the Wyoming State Penal Institution.

IT IS FURTHER ORDERED that if deemed appropriate by the Department of Immigration and Naturalization Services, the Defendant shall be immediately deported and returned to Mexico.

Figure 5-4

---

[5] To verify these facts please read *United States v. Chavez-Diaz*, 444 F.3d 1223 (10th Cir. 2006).

Now you are probably saying to yourself, "I don't have a case in Wyoming, so this method does not apply to me." But that is untrue. Whether you have a federal case or a case in a state other than Wyoming, this method *does* apply to you. The key to this method is to understand that you and your defense attorney can ask for certain provisions in a plea agreement. That is why it is called "plea negotiations." It is a give and take process. Ultimately, the prosecutor is trying to obtain a conviction, negotiate a just sentence, and avoid the expense of a trial and lengthy appeal process. You, as a defendant, can assist him with this endeavor. However, you should be adequately compensated for your assistance. Let us examine some ways in which you and your attorney could negotiate a favorable plea agreement.

A person is in the country illegally. He has just been arrested by North Carolina authorities and found to be in possession of a firearm. The state police contact federal authorities in Raleigh, North Carolina. The person is charged in federal court with two crimes; illegal re-entry and being an illegal alien in possession of a firearm. Unfortunately, he is in a federal district that does not offer fast-track departures to people charged with crimes other than illegal re-entry. A preliminary presentence report is developed in which the person's offense level (after a 3-level reduction for acceptance of responsibility) is found to be 27 and his criminal history category is II. This produced an advisory guideline range of 78 to 97 months of imprisonment. However, the validity of the traffic stop is in question. If the person files a motion to suppress the evidence, he *may* be able to win his claim and have the firearm suppressed. At the bare minimum, the federal prosecutor will have to call at least 3 witnesses at the evidentiary hearing and spend money preparing and presenting the evidence. During plea negotiations, the U.S. Attorney's Office refuses to dismiss either of the two counts. The defendant, on the other hand, tells his attorney that he feels that a 3-level reduction for acceptance of responsibility does not adequately compensate him for all that he must sacrifice (78 to 97 months versus 108 to 135, without acceptance of responsibility). The defense attorney goes back to the negotiating table. He tells the prosecutor that he feels that the government should reduce his client's offense level by two, which would give him an advisory guideline range of 63 to 78 months, because his client would be ineligible for any early release programs offered by the BOP. This action, he tells the federal prosecutor, would eliminate any unwarranted sentencing disparity. In exchange, the defendant agrees to plead guilty, forego his suppression hearing and appeals, and submit to a streamlined immigration removal process. This is essentially the fast track process in all but name.

Moreover, if the U.S. Attorney in your case is adverse to a similar reduction, your defense attorney can always ask the U.S. Attorney's Office to develop a letter stating that it would not be opposed to the U.S. Attorney General granting you immigration early release. This letter would then be used to support a later request for immigration early release. This support can be crucial. Earlier in this book, you learned about a federal prisoner who had transferred from an Arizona state prison. When he sought immigration early release, the Attorney General sought a recommendation from the warden. Then, based on the warden's negative comments, the Attorney General ultimately denied the prisoner's request. If that same prisoner had had a positive recommendation letter from the U.S. Attorney's Office, it's doubtful that the Attorney General would have even contacted the warden before granting the prisoner early release.

The above negotiation strategies are but two of the many ways that federal defendants and their attorneys can seek a lower sentence and/or immigration early release. If you are a federal non-U.S. citizen defendant, your attorney, *at the very least*, should be seeking to get the U.S. Attorney's Office to develop an immigration early release letter on your behalf.

Similarly, there are a number of ways state prisoners can seek the same benefits. First and foremost, you should have your defense attorney obtain an immigration early release letter from the District Attorney's Office. If you maintain good conduct during your prison term, this letter may encourage the parole board to grant your parole or the governor to commute your sentence.

Here is yet another example of how a state defendant can be granted early release—without doing one day in state or federal prison. A Nigerian national was arrested in Mississippi by a deputy sheriff with the Lauderdale County Sheriff's Department. The person's arrest triggered an alert in ICE's computer database and an I-147 form was sent to the county sheriff's department, placing a hold or detainer on the person. Because of his prior drug conviction and removal order, both the defendant and his attorney knew he was removable from the country. With permission from his client, defense counsel negotiated a plea deal in which the defendant would plead guilty to one count of possession of a firearm by a felon. In exchange, the D.A. agreed to a 10-year sentence, with 9 years and 364 days suspended, and post-release supervision for a period of 5 years. Importantly, the defendant would immediately be placed in the custody of ICE so that he could be deported. The plea agreement also stated that if the defendant violated the conditions of his post-release supervision—namely, illegally returning to the U.S.—the court would impose the suspended sentence (9 years and 364 days) and place him in the custody of the Mississippi Department of Corrections.

The Circuit Court for the 10th District accepted the plea agreement and sentenced the defendant to the exact terms in the plea agreement. The defendant spent 5 days in the Lauderdale County Detention Facility in Meridian, Mississippi before ICE agents took custody of him.

In total, the defendant spent 148 days in the county jail; 143 days before he was sentenced and 5 days after he was sentenced. That is only 4.05% of his sentence (148 days out of 3,649 days). As you can see, this defendant's rate of incarceration (4.05%) was similar to the rate of incarceration served in the Wyoming case (3.15% to 4.72%). It also saved the state of Mississippi about $360,000 in incarceration costs and gave the people of Mississippi peace of mind, because the defendant is out of the country and cannot cause any more trouble in that state. And if he returns to the U.S. and is arrested, he will be extradited back to Mississippi to complete his suspended sentence in state prison (in addition to the federal illegal re-entry sentence he will face).[6]

The state of Illinois has even more favorable laws because it gives a non-U.S. citizen defendant two opportunities to get out of jail before he or she serves a prison sentence. Under Public Act 097-0697, section 5-5-3(l)(A), a non-violent defendant who commits a felony or misdemeanor offense can ask the district attorney to file a motion with the court to hold his or her sentence in abeyance and remand him or her to the immediate custody of ICE. See Figure 5-5. This can be done if a final order of removal has already been issued by ICE. The sentence will not begin to run unless the person returns to the U.S. illegally and is apprehended. At that point, the person will have to serve the entire sentence and will be ineligible for sentence credit for good

---

[6] Similarly, in *Commonwealth of Kentucky v. Guevara-Barcenas*, Case No. 07-CR-540, in Fayette (Kentucky) Circuit Court, Guevara was convicted of assault in the third degree on May 30, 2007 and given a 1-year sentence. He was taken into ICE custody and deported on August 3, 2007.

conduct. Pursuant to section 5-5-3(l)(B), if no final order of removal has been issued by the time the defendant is sentenced, he or she can later ask (after the removal order has been issued) the district attorney to file a motion with the court asking that the sentence be suspended and that he or she be committed to ICE's custody. See Figure 5-6. The sentence would stop running at that point. However, it would start to run again if the person returned to the U.S. illegally and was apprehended. The alien defendant would have to serve his or her total sentence (minus any time served before the sentence was suspended) and would be ineligible for any sentence credit for good conduct. See Figure 5-7.

As this chapter demonstrates, there are numerous ways in which a non-U.S. citizen defendant can reduce or even avoid a prison sentence. Thus, be sure to explore these avenues with your defense attorney before you sign or accept any plea deal.

Illinois Public Act 097-0697
Section 5-5-3(l)(A)

(1) (A) Except as provided in paragraph (C) of subsection (1), whenever a defendant, who is an alien as defined by the Immigration and Nationality Act, is convicted of any felony or misdemeanor offense, the court after sentencing the defendant may, upon motion of the State's Attorney, hold sentence in abeyance and remand the defendant to the custody of the Attorney General of the United States or his or her designated agent to be deported when:

(1) a final order of deportation has been issued against the defendant pursuant to proceedings under the immigration and Nationality Act, and

(2) the deportation of the defendant would not deprecate the seriousness of the defendant's conduct and would not be inconsistent with the ends of justice. Otherwise, the defendant shall be sentenced as provided in this Chapter V.

Figure 5-5

Illinois Public Act 097-0697
Section 5-5-3(l)(B)

(B) If the defendant has already been sentenced for a felony or misdemeanor offense, or has been placed on probation under Section 10 of the Cannabis Control Act, Section 410 of the Illinois Controlled Substances Act, or Section 70 of the Methamphetamine Control and Community Protection Act, the court may, upon motion of the State's Attorney to suspend the sentence imposed, commit the defendant to the custody of the Attorney General of the United States or his or her designated agent when:

(1) a final order of deportation has been issued against the defendant pursuant to proceedings under the immigration and Nationality Act, and

(2) the deportation of the defendant would not deprecate the seriousness of the defendant's conduct and would not be inconsistent with the ends of justice.

Figure 5-6

Illinois Public Act 097-0697
Section 5-5-3(l)(D)

(D) Upon motion of the State's Attorney, if a defendant sentenced under this Section returns to the jurisdiction of the United States, the defendant shall be recommitted to the custody of the county from which he or she was sentenced. Thereafter, the defendant shall be brought before the sentencing court, which may impose any sentence that was available under Section 5-5-3 at the time of initial sentencing. In addition, the defendant shall not be eligible for additional sentence credit for good conduct as provided under Section 3-6-3.

Figure 5-7

APPENDIX H
(CONNECTICUT LAW ON DEPORTATION PAROLE)

2012 Connecticut General Statutes
Title 54 - Criminal Procedure
Chapter 961 - Trial and Proceedings After Conviction
Section 54-125d - Deportation parole of aliens.

Universal Citation: CT Gen Stat § 54-125d

(a) The Board of Pardons and Paroles shall enter into an agreement with the United States Immigration and Naturalization Service for the deportation of parolees who are aliens as described in 8 USC 1252a(b)(2) and for whom an order of deportation has been issued pursuant to 8 USC 1252(b) or 8 USC 1252a(b).

(b) The Department of Correction shall determine those inmates who shall be referred to the Board of Pardons and Paroles based on intake interviews by the department and standards set forth by the United States Immigration and Naturalization Service for establishing immigrant status.

(c) Notwithstanding the provisions of subdivision (2) of subsection (b) of section 54-125a, any person whose eligibility for parole is restricted under said subdivision shall be eligible for deportation parole under this section after having served fifty per cent of the definite sentence imposed by the court.

(d) Notwithstanding any provision of the general statutes, a sentencing court may refer any person convicted of an offense other than a capital felony under the provisions of section 53a-54b in effect prior to April 25, 2012, or a class A felony who is an alien to the Board of Pardons and Paroles for deportation under this section.

(e) Any person who is approved for deportation under this section shall have his sentence placed in a hold status for a period of ten years. If the parolee reenters the United States within such ten-year period, he shall be in violation of his parole agreement, the remainder of his sentence shall be reinstated and he shall be ineligible for parole consideration.

(f) Any person approved for deportation parole shall not be eligible for any form of bond whether by the state or the federal government. Any person approved for deportation parole shall be transferred to the United States Immigration and Naturalization Service for deportation in accordance with the agreement entered into pursuant to subsection (a) of this section. Any person approved for deportation parole shall waive all rights to appeal his conviction, extradition and deportation.

(P.A. 97-256, S. 1; P.A. 04-234, S. 2; P.A. 12-5, S. 33.)

History: P.A. 04-234 replaced Board of Parole with Board of Pardons and Paroles, effective July 1, 2004; P.A. 12-5 amended Subsec. (d) to add reference to provisions of Sec. 53a-54b in effect prior to April 25, 2012, re conviction of a capital felony, effective April 25, 2012.

APPENDIX I
(COLORADO LAW ON DEPORTATION PAROLE)

2016 Colorado Revised Statutes
Title 17 - Corrections
Correctional Facilities and Programs
Article 22.5 - Inmate and Parole Time Computation
Part 4 - Parole Eligibility and Discharge From Custody
§ 17-22.5-404.7. Presumption of parole - nonviolent offenders with ICE detainers

Universal Citation: CO Rev Stat § 17-22.5-404.7

(1) There shall be a presumption, subject to the final discretion of the parole board, in favor of granting parole to an inmate who has reached his or her parole eligibility date and who:

(a) Has been assessed by the Colorado risk assessment scale developed pursuant to section 17-22.5-404 (2) (a), to be medium risk or below of reoffense;

(b) Is not serving a sentence for a felony crime described in section 18-3-303, 18-3-306, or 18-6-701, C.R.S.; sections 18-7-402 to 18-7-407, C.R.S.; or section 18-12-102 or 18-12-109, C.R.S.; section 18-17-104, C.R.S., or section 18-18-407, C.R.S.; or a felony crime listed in section 24-4.1-302 (1), C.R.S.; and

(c) Has an active detainer lodged by the United States immigration and customs enforcement agency.

(2) In determining whether to grant parole pursuant to provisions of subsection (1) of this section, the board shall consider the cost of incarceration to the state of Colorado in relation

to the needs of further confinement of the inmate to achieve the purpose of the inmate's sentence.

(3) (a) The state board of parole may release an eligible inmate, pursuant to subsection (1) of this section, only to the custody of the United States immigration and customs enforcement agency or other law enforcement agency with authority to execute the detainer on behalf of the United States immigration and customs enforcement agency.

(b) If the United States immigration and customs enforcement agency withdraws the detainer or declines to take the inmate into custody, the state board of parole shall hold a recission hearing to reconsider the granting of parole to the inmate.

(c) If the United States immigration and customs enforcement agency issues an order of deportation for the inmate, the department of corrections shall submit a request to the state board of parole to discharge parole.

(d) A denial of parole by the state board of parole pursuant to this section shall not affect an inmate's eligibility for another form of parole or release applicable under law.

(4) The board may consider the application for parole pursuant to the proceedings set forth in section 17-2-201 (4) (f) or 17-2-201 (9) (a).

(5) For inmates who were parole eligible before May 23, 2011, the department shall notify the state board of parole of any of those inmates who meet the criteria listed in subsection (1) of this section, and the board shall either set a release hearing or conduct a release review within ninety days after May 23, 2011.

APPENDIX J
(SAMPLE TEXAS APPLICATION FOR COMMUTATION OF SENTENCE)

COS-10 (R-01/11/2010)   Date: _____
(Last Name, First and Middle Name)

_____   _____

APPLICATION FOR COMMUTATION OF SENTENCE TO THE TEXAS BOARD OF PARDONS & PAROLES

TO THE BOARD OF PARDONS AND PAROLES OF TEXAS:

I hereby request the Board of Pardons and Paroles or its designated agent to file this application for Clemency, to investigate the statements herein made under oath and, if the facts so justify, make a favorable recommendation to the Governor of the State of Texas that a Commutation of Sentence, to which I may be entitled under the laws of the State of Texas, be granted.

A.   DEMOGRAPHIC INFORMATION

Current full name	Last Name	☐ Jr. ☐ III ☐ Sr. ☐ IV	First Name	Full Middle Name
Name(s) convicted under				
Race and sex	Race _____ Sex _____			
Date and place of birth	Date of birth _____ Place of birth _____			
Driver's license	State _____ License Number _____			
Alias names (including maiden name, name by former marriage and nicknames), birth dates, social security #'s, etc.				
Current marital status	☐ Married – Spouse's Name: _____			
	☐ Divorced ☐ Separated ☐ Single			
Children / support / alimony	I have _____ children under the age of 18 years. I am supporting the following named children under the age of 18 years: _____ I currently pay $ _____ / month in child support. I currently pay $ _____ / month in alimony.			

The Early Release Provision / David Mathis

B.   ADDRESSES

Current Mailing Address		Current Physical Address	
Indicate your current mailing address.		*Provide information even if the physical and mailing addresses are the same.*	
Number and street	Apartment	Number and street	Apartment
City	State Zip Code	City	State Zip Code
Home phone number [_____] _____		County of residence _____	
Work phone number [_____] _____		Years resided at physical residence _____	
Email Address _____			

Previous Addresses

List **all** previous physical addresses since age 18. Do not use post office boxes. If you lived in an apartment complex, list your apartment number. *All time periods must be accounted for.* Include complete dates (months and years of residence), addresses, city, state and zip codes. Complete this page before attaching any additional page(s). Place attachments behind this page.

From (month/year):	Number and street		Apartment
To (month/year):	City	State	Zip Code

From (month/year):	Number and street		Apartment
To (month/year):	City	State	Zip Code

From (month/year):	Number and street		Apartment
To (month/year):	City	State	Zip Code

From (month/year):	Number and street		Apartment
To (month/year):	City	State	Zip Code

122

The Early Release Provision / David Mathis

C.   EMPLOYMENT

Please give a comprehensive adult (since age 18) employment history, beginning with your present employment and working backwards. Include employer's name, address, your job position working title, description of job duties, salary, dates employed, and reason for leaving. Complete this page before attaching any additional page(s). Place attachments behind this page.

From (month/year):	Employer name
To (month/year):	Employer address
Job position (working title)	Description of your work duties
Average monthly salary	Reason for leaving

From (month/year):	Employer name
To (month/year):	Employer address
Job position (working title)	Description of your work duties
Average monthly salary	Reason for leaving

From (month/year):	Employer name
To (month/year):	Employer address
Job position (working title)	Description of your work duties
Average monthly salary	Reason for leaving

From (month/year):	Employer name
To (month/year):	Employer address
Job position (working title)	Description of your work duties
Average monthly salary	Reason for leaving

The Early Release Provision / David Mathis

_____

D.   STATUS

Are you currently incarcerated in a Texas penal institution? *If "yes," list your (TDCJ-CID) identification number.*	☐ Yes ☐ No ID number: _____
Were you ever incarcerated in a Texas penal institution? *If "yes," list all (TDCJ-CID) identification numbers.*	☐ Yes ☐ No Prior ID number: _____ Prior ID number: _____
Are you currently serving a term of probation? *If "yes", identify the county of current residence, name and phone number of your probation officer.*	☐ Yes ☐ No County: _____ Name: _____ Number: (___) _____
Are you currently on parole, annual report status, or serving a term of mandatory supervision? *If "yes," identify the county of current residence.*	☐ Yes ☐ No County: _____
Do you have any pending criminal charges? *If "yes," attach an explanation page. Place the attachment behind this page.*	☐ Yes ☐ No
Have you been incarcerated in a federal or non-Texas state institution? *If "yes," list all identification numbers. Include the facility name and location.*	☐ Yes ☐ No ID Number: _____ Institution: _____ Location: _____

The Early Release Provision / David Mathis

_____

E.   JUSTIFICATION FOR CLEMENCY CONSIDERATION

(1)   State the reasons and circumstances for requesting a commutation of sentence.

Complete this page before attaching any additional page(s). Place any attachments immediately behind this page.

125

The Early Release Provision / David Mathis

_____

F.   CERTIFICATION BY APPLICANT

Please read the following statements carefully and indicate your understanding and acceptance by signing in the space provided. This application must be signed.

I hereby give my permission to the Board of Pardons and Paroles or its designated agent to make any inquiry and receive any information of record that it may deem proper in the investigation of this application for clemency; and

I understand that compliance with these requirements is sufficient for the Board's consideration of this application, but compliance does not necessarily mean that favorable action will result.

I hereby swear upon my oath that I am the subject herein named and the facts contained in this application are true and correct.

_____
Applicant's Signature (Full Name)

_____
Date

CHAPTER 6
RETURNING TO THE UNITED STATES

Before closing this book, there is one key aspect about the immigration early release program that you must be made aware of. It deals with the potential punishment you may receive if you illegally return to the United States after you have been deported.

There are serious consequences for a federal or state prisoner who has been deported under the program and who later returns to the U.S. The person essentially faces two punishments. First, the person will have to complete the remainder of his or her previous sentence. For instance, let us say that a person was serving a 4-year state sentence in Georgia. The person completed two years of his sentence   before   he   was   deported   pursuant   to section 1231(a)(4)(B)(ii). Three years later, the person illegally returns to the United States and is arrested in Texas. He will be extradited to Georgia to complete the final two years of his previous state sentence. That is the first punishment. Second, the person also faces punishment under federal law. Title 8, United States Code, section 1326(b)(4), for example, reads, in relevant parts, that: "in the case of any alien . . . who was removed from the United States pursuant to [8 U.S.C. section 1231(a)(4)(B)] who thereafter, without permission of the [U.S.] Attorney General, enters, attempts to enter, or is at any time found in, the United States . . . shall be . . . imprisoned for not more than 10 years." See Figure 6-1. Simply stated, any person who has been deported under section 1231(a)(4)(B) and illegally returns to the U.S., faces up to 10 years in federal prison. But only if the person has not previously been convicted of an "aggravated felony." A person with such a conviction would face imprisonment for "not more than 20 years" under section 1326(b)(2).

As the list in Figure 6-2 and 6-2(a) shows, the term "aggravated felony" has a broad meaning—from murder to theft to gambling.[7] And remember, that while this list contains federal offenses, if you have a similar type of state conviction, it will be counted as an aggravated felony during your federal prosecution for illegal re-entry. That simple action will double your potential sentence from 10 years to 20 years, which will be served after you have completed the remainder of your previous federal or state sentence.

Some states also preclude prisoners who violate the terms of the program from early parole release and future early parole release. In Connecticut, the prisoner's sentence is placed on "hold" status for 10 years. If the person unlawfully returns within 10 years, he or she

---

[7] The list in Figure 6-2 and 6-2(a) is more extensive than the one in Figure 4-2, which list non-violent crimes that make state prisoners ineligible for immigration early release under 8 U.S.C. § 1231(a)(4)(B)(ii). If you are convicted for any of the crimes listed in Figure 6-2 and 6-2(a), you may be "removable" under 8 U.S.C. § 1227(a).

must serve the remainder of his or her sentence and is ineligible for parole consideration.

Most states, however, do not have a time limitation. In North Carolina, a deported former prisoner who returns to the U.S. at any time after release must serve "for a period equal to the inmate's maximum sentence" and is "not eligible for any future release under this section."

Enhanced Penalty Provision
(Title 8, United States Code, Section 1326)

§ 1326. Reentry of removed aliens

(a) **In general.** Subject to subsection (b), any alien who—
(1) has been denied admission, excluded, deported, or removed or has departed the United States while an order of exclusion, deportation, or removal is outstanding, and thereafter
(2) enters, attempts to enter, or is at any time found in, the United States, unless (A) prior to his re-embarkation at a place outside the United States or his application for admission from foreign contiguous territory, the Attorney General has expressly consented to such alien's reapplying for admission; or (B) with respect to an alien previously denied admission and removed, unless such alien shall establish that he was not required to obtain such advance consent under this or any prior Act,

shall be fined under title 18, United States Code, or imprisoned not more than 2 years or both.

(b) **Criminal penalties for reentry of certain removed aliens.** Notwithstanding subsection (a), in the case of any alien described in such subsection—
(1) whose removal was subsequent to a conviction for commission of three or more misdemeanors involving drugs, crimes against the person, or both, or a felony (other than an aggravated felony), such alien shall be fined under title 18, United States Code, imprisoned not more than 10 years, or both;
(2) whose removal was subsequent to a conviction for commission of an aggravated felony, such alien shall be fined under such title, imprisoned not more than 20 years, or both;
(3) who has been excluded from the United States pursuant to section 235(c) [8 USCS § 1225(c)] because the alien was excludable under section 212(a)(3)(B) [8 USCS § 1182(a)(3)(B)] or who has been removed from the United States pursuant to the provisions of title V [8 USCS §§ 1531 et seq.], and who thereafter, without the permission of the Attorney General, enters the United States, or attempts to do so, shall be fined under title 18, United States Code, and imprisoned for a period of 10 years, which sentence shall not run concurrently with any other sentence.[;] or
(4) who was removed from the United States pursuant to section 241 (a)(4)(B) [8 USCS § 1231(a)(4)(B)] who thereafter, without the permission of the Attorney General, enters, attempts to enter, or is at any time found in, the United States (unless the Attorney General has expressly consented to such alien's reentry) shall be fined under title 18, United States Code, imprisoned for not more than 10 years, or both.

Figure 6-1

**Aggravated Felonies Under Federal Law
(Title 8, United States Code, § 1101 (a)(43))**

(43) The term "aggravated felony" means—

(A) murder, rape, or sexual abuse of a minor;

(B) illicit trafficking in a controlled substance (as defined in section 102 of the Controlled Substances Act [21 USCS § 802]), including a drug trafficking crime (as defined in section 924(c) of title 18, United States Code);

(C) illicit trafficking in firearms or destructive devices (as defined in section 921 of title 18, United States Code) or in explosive materials (as defined in section 841 (c) of that title);

(D) an offense described in section 1956 of title 18, United States Code (relating to laundering of monetary instruments) or section 1957 of that title (relating to engaging in monetary transactions in property derived from specific unlawful activity) if the amount of the funds exceeded $10,000;

(E) an offense described in—

    (i) section 842 (h) or (i) oftitle 18, United States Code, or section 844 (d), (e), (f), (g), (h), or (i) of that title (relating to explosive materials offenses);

    (ii) section 922(g) (1), (2), (3), (4), or (5), (j), (n), (o), (p), or (r) or 924 (b) or (h) of title 18, United States Code (relating to firearms offenses); or

    (iii) section 5861 of the Internal Revenue Code of 1986 [26 USCS § 5861] (relating to firearms offenses);

(F) a crime of violence (as defined in section 16 of title 18, United States Code, but not including a purely political offense) for which the term of imprisonment [is] at least one year;

(G) a theft offense (including receipt of stolen property) or burglary offense for which the term of imprisonment [is] at least one year;

(H) an offense described in section 875, 876, 877, or 1202 of title 18, United States Code (relating to the demand for or receipt of ransom);

(I) an offense described in section 2251, 2251A, or 2252 of title 18, United States Code (relating to child pornography);

(J) an offense described in section 1962 of title 18, United States Code (relating to racketeer influenced corrupt organizations), or an offense described in section 1084 (if it is a second or subsequent offense) or 1955 of that title (relating to gambling offenses), for which a sentence of one year imprisonment or more may be imposed;

(K) an offense that—

(i) relates to the owning, controlling, managing, or supervising of a prostitution business;

(ii) is described in section 2421,2422, or 2423 of title 18, United States Code (relating to transportation for the purpose of prostitution) if committed for commercial advantage; or

Figure 6-2

(iii) is described in any of sections 1581-1585 or 1588-1591 of title 18, United States Code (relating to peonage, slavery, involuntary servitude, and trafficking in persons);

(L) an offense described in—

(i) section 793 (relating to gathering or transmitting national defense information), 798 (relating to disclosure of classified information), 2153 (relating to sabotage) or 2381 or 2382 (relating to treason) of title 18, United States Code;

(ii) section 601 of the National Security Act of 1947 [50 USCS § 421] (relating to protecting the identity of undercover intelligence agents);

(iii) section 601 of the National Security Act of 1947 [50 USCS § 421] (relating to protecting the identity of undercover agents);

(M) an offense that—

(i) involves fraud or deceit in which the loss to the victim or victims exceeds $10,000; or

(ii) is described in section 7201 of the Internal Revenue Code of 1986 [26 USCS § 7201] (relating to tax evasion) in which the revenue loss to the Government exceeds $10,000;

(N) an offense described in paragraph (1)(A) or (2) of section 274(a) [8 USCS § 1324(a)(I)(A) or (2)] (relating to alien smuggling), except in the case of a first offense for which the alien has affirmatively shown that the alien committed the offense for the purpose of assisting, abetting, or aiding only the alien's spouse, child, or parent (and no other individual) to violate a provision of this Act[;]

(O) an offense described in section 275(a) or 276 [8 USCS § 1325(a) or 1326] committed by an alien who was previously deported on the basis of a conviction for an offense described in another subparagraph of this paragraph;

(P) an offense (i) which either is falsely making, forging, counterfeiting, mutilating, or altering a passport or instrument in violation of section 1543 of title 18, United States Code, or is described in section 1546(a) of such title (relating to document fraud) and (ii) for which the term of imprisonment is at least 12 months, except in the case of a first offense for which the alien has affirmatively shown that the alien committed the offense for the purpose of assisting, abetting, or aiding only the alien's spouse, child, or parent (and no other individual) to violate a provision of this Act;

(Q) an offense relating to a failure to appear by a defendant for service of sentence if the underlying offense is punishable by imprisonment for a term of 5 years or more;

(R) an offense relating to commercial bribery, counterfeiting, forgery, or trafficking in vehicles the identification numbers of which have been altered for which the term of imprisonment is at least one year;

(S) an offense relating to obstruction of justice, perjury or subornation of perjury, or bribery of a witness, for which the term of imprisonment is at least one year;

(T) an offense relating to a failure to appear before a court pursuant to a court order to answer to or dispose of a charge of a felony for which a sentence of 2 years' imprisonment or more may be imposed; and

(U) an attempt or conspiracy to commit an offense described in this paragraph.

Figure 6-2(a)

You are not being provided with this penalty information as a means to scare you. Indeed, in reality, people are usually sentenced to far less than 20 years (between 5 years and 10 years) if they have a prior aggravated felony and illegally return to the U.S.[8] Still, 5 years is a lengthy sentence to serve (even in a federal prison) simply for illegally returning to the U.S. And believe me, federal prisons are not the "Club Fed" that everyone imagines. In fact, some federal prisons don't even have microwaves (and stingers are prohibited). Based on these considerations, you need this information to better assess whether returning to the U.S. after you have been deported is worth the risk.

In Appendix K, you will see a copy of an actual federal plea agreement. In the case, the person was charged with reentry of a removed alien, in violation of Title 8, United States Code, section 1326. On August 6, 2015, the person entered into a "fast-track" plea agreement with the U.S. Attorney's Office. Under the terms of the plea agreement, the person agreed to plead guilty to the charge illegal reentry. In addition, he agreed to reinstatement of removal proceedings, and waived any appellate and collateral attacks to his sentence.

In exchange, the U.S. Attorney's Office agreed to seek a two or three-level reduction in the person's offense level for acceptance of responsibility and a two or four-level departure under the Early Disposition ("fast-track") Program.

On November 2, 2015, the person appeared in the district court for sentencing. The judge found that his base offense level was 8. At that level, the person would have been sentenced to 12 months or less. However, because he had a prior aggravated felony conviction (a California drug trafficking conviction), the court

---

[8] If your attorney has to negotiate a plea deal, have him or her try to get the prosecutor to drop any charges that would be considered an aggravated felony. See Figure 6-2. If this is not possible, try to get the prosecutor to reduce the charge. California Penal Code § 496, receipt of stolen property, is an aggravated felony under federal law. However, § 490.2 (petty theft) and § 484(a)(petty theft with prior conviction) are not.

enhanced his offense level by 16 levels, which gave him a new offense level of 24. The judge then granted the person a three-level reduction, which produced an adjusted offense level of 21. At that level the person's Guidelines range was 57 to 71 months. Thus, this person's sentence range went from 1-year or less to 5 years or more; all because the person had a prior drug arrest. The same thing would have occurred if the person had previously participated in the immigration early release program under section 1231(a)(4)(B). And remember, the district court judge can sentence a person up to 10 years in federal prison, regardless of what the Guidelines range is, if the person has participated in the immigration early release program and up to 20 years if he or she has a prior aggravated felony conviction.

APPENDIX K
(FEDERAL PLEA AGREEMENT)

Case 2:15-cr-00969-SPL   Document 26   Filed 11/02/15   Page 1 of 10

1 JOHN S. LEONARDO
   United States Attorney
2 District of Arizona
   CAROLINA ESCALANTE
3 Assistant U.S. Attorney
   Arizona State Bar No. 026238
4 Two Renaissance Square
   40 N. Central Ave., Suite 1200
5 Phoenix, Arizona 85004
   Telephone: 602-514-7500
6 Email: Fernanda.Escalante@usdoj.gov

7   IN THE UNITED STATES DISTRICT COURT

8   FOR THE DISTRICT OF ARIZONA

9
   United States of America,
10   No. CR-15-00969-PHX-NVW
               Plaintiff,
11   Mag. No. 15-08340 MJ
        v.
12   PLEA AGREEMENT
   Jesus Guadalupe Vasquez Ayala,
13 a.k.a.: Jorge Galvan-Ortega,   (Fast Track 5K3.1)
   a.k.a.: Alfredo Ayala-Gomez,
14 a.k.a.: Guadalupe Vasquez Ayala,
   a.k.a.: Jesus Guadalupe Vasquez-Ayala,
15 a.k.a.: Juan Carlos Cotacota,

16   Defendant.

17   The United States of America and the defendant hereby agree to dispose of this

18 matter on the following terms and conditions:

19   PLEA

20   The defendant will plead guilty to an Information charging a violation of Title 8,

21 United States Code (U.S.C.), Section 1326(a), with a possible sentencing enhancement

22 under 1326(b)(1) or 1326(b)(2), Reentry of Removed Alien.

23 1.   MAXIMUM PENALTIES

24   a.   A violation of 8 U.S.C. § 1326(a), a Class E felony, is punishable by a

25 maximum term of imprisonment of 2 years, a maximum fine of $250,000, or both

26 imprisonment and a fine, and a term of supervised release of up to 1 year. If a sentencing

27 enhancement under 8 U.S.C. § 1326(b)(1), a Class C felony, is applicable, then the

28 maximum term of imprisonment is 10 years. If the sentencing enhancement under 8

136

1   U.S.C. § 1326(b)(2), a Class C felony, is applicable, then the maximum term of

2   imprisonment is 20 years. A Class C felony is punishable by both imprisonment and a

3   maximum fine of $250,000, and a term of supervised release of up to 3 years.

4   b.   According to the United States Sentencing Guidelines (U.S.S.G.) issued

5   pursuant to the Sentencing Reform Act of 1984, the Court shall:

6   (1)   Order the defendant to pay a fine pursuant to 18 U.S.C. §§ 3572 and

7   3553, unless the Court finds that a fine is not appropriate; and

8   (2)   Order the defendant to serve a term of supervised release when

9   required by statute or when a sentence of imprisonment of more than one year is

10   imposed, and may impose a term of supervised release in all other cases.

11   c.   Pursuant to 18 U.S.C. § 3013(a)(2)(A), the Court is required to order the

12   defendant to pay a $100 special assessment.

13   2.   AGREEMENTS REGARDING SENTENCING

14   a.   Stipulation: Acceptance of Responsibility. Pursuant to Fed. R. Crim. P.

15   11(c)(1)(C), if the defendant makes full and complete disclosure to the U.S. Probation

16   Office of the circumstances surrounding the defendant's commission of the offense, and

17   if the defendant demonstrates an acceptance of responsibility for this offense up to and

18   including the time of sentencing, the United States will stipulate and agree to a two-level

19   reduction pursuant to U.S.S.G. § 3E1.1. If the defendant has an offense level of 16 or

20   more, the United States will stipulate and agree to an additional one-level reduction

21   pursuant to U.S.S.G. § 3E1.1.

22   b.   Stipulated Sentence Under Early Disposition Program.   Although the

23   parties understand that the Sentencing Guidelines are only advisory, and just one of the

24   factors the Court will consider under 18 U.S.C. § 3553(a), pursuant to Fed. R. Crim. P.

25   11(c)(1)(C) and U.S.S.G. § 5K3.1, the United States and the defendant stipulate and

26   agree that the following is an appropriate disposition of this case:

27   The defendant's Base Offense Level will be calculated as the sum of Offense

28   Level 8 PLUS the sentencing guideline adjustment for the defendant's most serious prior

- 2 -

1 conviction, pursuant to U.S.S.G § 2L1.2(a) and (b), as determined by the Court at the

2 time of sentencing. Defendant's Offense Level will be further reduced pursuant to the

3 Attorney General's Early Disposition Program as follows:

4   (1)   A two-level departure if the defendant is in criminal history category

5 VI or has at least one felony conviction for an offense identified in U.S.S.G. §

6 2L1.2(b)(1)(A) [a drug trafficking offense for which the sentence imposed exceeded 13

7 months; a crime of violence; a firearms offense; a child pornography offense; a national

8 security or terrorism offense; a human trafficking offense; or an alien smuggling offense],

9 and a stipulation that defendant's sentence shall not exceed the high-end of the final

10 advisory Sentencing Guideline range. If the defendant requests, or if the Court

11 authorizes, any adjustments or departures pursuant to the Sentencing Guidelines, the

12 United States may withdraw from this agreement. However, nothing in this agreement

13 shall preclude the defendant from arguing for, or the Court from granting, a variance

14 under 18 U.S.C. §3553(a) in support of a sentence below the final advisory Sentencing

15 Guideline range. The United States reserves the right to oppose any variance.

16   (2)   A four-level departure and a stipulation that the defendant's sentence

17 shall be within the final advisory Sentencing Guideline range if the defendant has a

18 felony conviction that does not meet the criteria of subparagraph (1) above. If the

19 defendant receives the four-level departure provided under this subparagraph, the parties

20 agree that it shall be the only reduction in sentence (other than for acceptance of

21 responsibility) that the defendant shall receive. The defendant understands and agrees

22 that if he requests or if the Court authorizes (a) any adjustments or departures pursuant to

23 the Sentencing Guidelines; (b) any variance under 18 U.S.C. §3553(a); or (c) other

24 reduction or adjustment of sentence not specifically agreed to in writing by the parties,

25 the United States may withdraw from the plea agreement.

26   (3)   If the defendant does not qualify for a 1326(b)(1) or 1326(b)(2)

27 enhancement, then in lieu of the departures listed in subparagraphs (1) and (2) above, the

28 defendant's sentence shall not exceed the following caps:

Three months of imprisonment if defendant's Criminal History Category is I;

Four months of imprisonment if defendant's Criminal History Category is II;

Five months of imprisonment if defendant's Criminal History Category is III;

Six months of imprisonment if the defendant's Criminal History Category is IV;

Nine months of imprisonment if defendant's Criminal History Category is V; and

Twelve months and one day of imprisonment if the defendant's Criminal History Category is VI.

c.   Multiple Offense Levels. If the defendant has multiple convictions, which fall under more than one specific offense classification level (i.e. U.S.S.G. § 2L1.2(b)(1)(A), (B), and/or (C)), the Sentencing Guidelines range shall be calculated using the highest specific offense classification level. The Court will determine the precise level of offense and advisory Sentencing Guideline range based upon the defendant's criminal record.

d.   Criminal History Points. If the defendant has 18 or more criminal history points, the United States shall have the right to withdraw from this agreement.

e.   No Other Agreements. This plea agreement contains all of the terms, conditions, and stipulations regarding sentencing. If the court departs from the terms and conditions set forth in this plea agreement, either party may withdraw.

f.   Supervised Release. If the defendant is on supervised release, the United States shall have the right to withdraw from this agreement.

3.   **COURT APPROVAL REQUIRED**

If the Court, after reviewing this plea agreement, concludes that any provision is inappropriate, it may reject the plea agreement under Fed. R. Crim. P. 11(c)(5), giving the defendant, in accordance with Fed. R. Crim. P. 11(d)(2)(A), an opportunity to withdraw the defendant's guilty plea.

4.   **WAIVER OF DEFENSES AND APPEAL RIGHTS**

The defendant waives (1) any and all motions, defenses, probable cause determinations, and objections that the defendant could assert to the indictment or

- 4 -

1 information; and (2) any right to file an appeal, any collateral attack, and any other writ
2 or motion that challenges the conviction, an order of restitution or forfeiture, the entry of
3 judgment against the defendant, or any aspect of the defendant's sentence, including the
4 manner in which the sentence is determined, including but not limited to any appeals
5 under 18 U.S.C. § 3742 (sentencing appeals) and motions under 28 U.S.C. §§ 2241 and
6 2255 (habeas petitions), and any right to file a motion for modification of sentence,
7 including under 18 U.S.C. § 3582(c). This waiver shall result in the dismissal of any
8 appeal, collateral attack, or other motion the defendant might file challenging the
9 conviction, order of restitution or forfeiture, or sentence in this case. This waiver shall
10 not be construed to bar an otherwise-preserved claim of ineffective assistance of counsel
11 or of "prosecutorial misconduct" (as that term is defined by Section II.B of Ariz. Ethics
12 Op. 15-01 (2015)).

13 **5.   REINSTATEMENT OF REMOVAL, DEPORTATION OR EXCLUSION
14 OR STIPULATION TO REMOVAL**

15 The defendant admits that the defendant was the subject of a previous order of
16 removal, deportation or exclusion. The defendant agrees to the reinstatement of that
17 previous order of removal, deportation or exclusion. The defendant admits that he does
18 not have a fear of returning to the country designated in the previous order. If this plea
19 agreement is accepted by the Court, the defendant agrees not to contest, either directly or
20 by collateral attack, the reinstatement of the prior order of removal, deportation or
21 exclusion.

22 **6.   PERJURY AND OTHER OFFENSES**

23 Nothing in this agreement shall be construed to protect the defendant in any way
24 from prosecution for perjury, false declaration or false statement, obstruction of justice,
25 or any other offense committed by the defendant after the date of this agreement. Any
26 information, statements, documents, or evidence the defendant provides to the United
27 States pursuant to this agreement, or to the Court, may be used against the defendant in
28 all such prosecutions.

- 5 -

7.   REINSTITUTION OF PROSECUTION

If the defendant's guilty plea is rejected, withdrawn, vacated, or reversed by any court in a later proceeding, the United States will be free to prosecute the defendant for all charges and/or allegations of supervised release violations as to which it has knowledge, and any charges and/or allegations of supervised release violations that have been dismissed or not alleged because of this plea agreement will be automatically reinstated. In such event, the defendant waives any objections, motions, or defenses based upon the Speedy Trial Act or the Sixth Amendment to the Constitution as to the delay occasioned by the later proceedings. Defendant agrees that the stipulated fast-track departures set forth under "Agreements Regarding Sentence" will not be offered if prosecution is re-instituted.

8.   DISCLOSURE OF INFORMATION

a.   The United States retains the unrestricted right to provide information and make any and all statements it deems appropriate to the Probation Office and to the Court in connection with the case.

b.   The defendant shall cooperate fully with the U.S. Probation Office. Such cooperation shall include providing complete and truthful responses to questions posed by the Probation Office including, but not limited to, questions relating to:

(1)   Criminal convictions, history of drug abuse and mental illness; and

(2)   Financial information, including present financial assets or liabilities that relate to the ability of the defendant to pay a fine.

9.   EFFECT ON OTHER PROCEEDINGS

This agreement does not preclude the United States from instituting any civil or administrative proceedings as may be appropriate now or in the future.

DEFENDANT'S APPROVAL AND ACCEPTANCE

I have read the entire plea agreement with the assistance of counsel and understand each of its provisions.

- 6 -

1   I have discussed the case and my constitutional and other rights with my attorney.

2   I understand that by entering my plea of guilty I shall waive my rights to plead not guilty;

3   to trial by jury; to confront, cross-examine, and compel the attendance of witnesses; to

4   present evidence in my defense; to remain silent and refuse to be a witness against myself

5   by asserting my privilege against self-incrimination; and to be presumed innocent until

6   proven guilty beyond a reasonable doubt, all with the assistance of counsel.

7   I agree to enter my guilty plea as indicated above on the terms and conditions set

8   forth in this agreement.

9   I have been advised by my attorney of the nature of the charges to which I am

10   entering my guilty plea. I have further been advised by my attorney of the nature and

11   range of the possible sentence and that my ultimate sentence shall be determined after

12   consideration of the advisory Sentencing Guidelines. I understand that the Sentencing

13   Guidelines are only advisory and that without this agreement the Court would be free to

14   exercise its discretion to impose any reasonable sentence up to the maximum set by

15   statute for the crimes of conviction.

16   My guilty plea is not the result of force, threats, assurances, or promises other than

17   the promises contained in this agreement. I agree to the provisions of this agreement as a

18   voluntary act on my part and I agree to be bound according to its provisions.

19   I fully understand that, if I am granted probation or placed on supervised release

20   by the Court, the terms and conditions of such probation/supervised release are subject to

21   modification at any time. I further understand that, if I violate any of the conditions of my

22   probation/supervised release, my probation/supervised release may be revoked and upon

23   such revocation, notwithstanding any other provision of this agreement, I may be

24   required to serve a term of imprisonment or my sentence may otherwise be altered.

25   I agree that this written plea agreement contains all the terms and conditions of my

26   plea. I further agree that promises, including any predictions as to the Sentencing

27   Guideline range or to any Sentencing Guideline factors that will apply, made by anyone

28

-7-

142

1   (including my attorney) that are not contained within this written plea agreement are null
2   and void and have no force and effect.
3   I am satisfied that my defense attorney has represented me in a competent manner.
4   I am fully capable of understanding the terms and conditions of this plea
5   agreement. I am not now using or under the influence of any drug, medication, liquor, or
6   other intoxicant or depressant that would impair my ability to fully understand the terms
7   and conditions of this plea agreement.

8   **ELEMENTS**
9   **Reentry of Removed Alien**
10 On or about November 9, 2014, in the District of Arizona:
11   1.   The defendant was an alien;
12   2.   The defendant had been previously denied admission, excluded, deported,
13 or removed from the United States;
14   3.   The defendant knowingly and voluntarily reentered or was present after a
15 voluntary entry and found in the United States in the District of Arizona; and
16   4.   The defendant did not obtain the express consent of the Attorney General or
17 the Secretary of Homeland Security to reapply for admission to the United States prior to
18 returning to the United States.

19 **FACTUAL BASIS**
20   I further admit the following facts are true and if this matter were to proceed to
21 trial the United States could prove the following facts beyond a reasonable doubt:
22
23 I am not a citizen or national of the United States. I was removed from the
24 United States through Nogales, Arizona, on December 29, 2003. I was
    voluntarily present and found in the United States at or near Phoenix,
    Arizona, on November 9, 2014. I did not obtain the express consent of the
25 United States government to reapply for admission to the United States
    prior to returning to the United States.
26 For sentencing purposes, I admit I was convicted of Possession or Purchase
27 for Sale of Designated Controlled Substances, a felony, on March 31, 2000,
    in the Superior Court of California, San Juaquin County. I was represented
28 by an attorney, and I was sentenced to two (2) years imprisonment.

- 8 -

143

1 I have read this agreement or it has been read to me in Spanish, and I have
2 carefully reviewed every part of it with my attorney. I understand it, and I voluntarily
3 agree to it.

4
5 ___7-22-15___   _Jesus GPe. Vazquez Ayala_
   Date   JESUS GUADALUPE VASQUEZ AYALA
6   Defendant

7

8   **DEFENSE ATTORNEY'S APPROVAL**
9
10 I have discussed this case and the plea agreement with my client in detail and have
11 advised the defendant of all matters within the scope of Fed. R. Crim. P. 11, the
12 constitutional and other rights of an accused, the factual basis for and the nature of the
13 offense to which the guilty plea will be entered, possible defenses, and the consequences
14 of the guilty plea including the maximum statutory sentence possible. I have discussed
15 the concept of the advisory Sentencing Guidelines with the defendant. No assurances,
16 promises, or representations that are not contained in this written agreement have been
17 given to me or to the defendant by the United States or any of its representatives. I have
18 concluded that the entry of the plea as indicated above on the terms and conditions set
19 forth in this agreement are in the best interests of my client. I agree to make a bona fide
20 effort to ensure that the guilty plea is entered in accordance with all the requirements of
   Fed. R. Crim. P. 11.
21 I translated or caused to be translated this agreement from English into Spanish to
22 the defendant on the __22 nd__ day of __July__, __2015__.
23
24
25 ___7-22-15___   _Baltazar Iniguez_
   Date   BALTAZAR INIGUEZ
26   Attorney for Defendant
27
28

                        - 9 -

                        144

The Early Release Provision / David Mathis

1

2   **UNITED STATES' APPROVAL**

3   I have reviewed this matter and the plea agreement. I agree on behalf of the

4   United States that the terms and conditions set forth are appropriate and are in the best

5   interests of justice.

6   JOHN S. LEONARDO
                                       United States Attorney
7   District of Arizona

8   Date 0/6/15

9   CAROLINA ESCALANTE
                                       Assistant U.S. Attorney
10

11   **COURT'S ACCEPTANCE**

12

13   3 NOV. 2015
     Date
14   Honorable Steven P. Logan
                                       United States District Judge
15

16

17

18

19

20

21

22

23

24

25

26

27

28

- 10 -

ACKNOWLEDGMENTS

There were a number of people who helped me in the development of this book. Indeed, there are too many to list here. Thus, I offer here a collective thank you to all of them.

In addition, I wish to offer a special thanks to the following people:

Jane Eichwald, at Ambler Document Processing Service, for her excellent typing skills and design layout. Any errors in this book are mine.

Jeffrey Lyons, Public Information Officer for the New Hampshire Department of Corrections, Office of the Commissioner. I thank you for answering each of my questions and providing me with a deeper understanding of New Hampshire law.

The staff in the Education Department at Federal Correctional Institution (FCI) Herlong. Thanks for the encouragement and providing me with the resources to complete this book.

Catrina M. Pavlik-Keenan and the rest of the staff at the Freedom of Information Act Office for the U.S. Immigration and

Customs Enforcement (ICE). The information that you provide proved invaluable to the completion of this book.

Lastly, James Springette and Annie Brown; without your emotional and financial support, this book would not have been possible.

ABOUT THE AUTHOR

David L. Mathis is a graduate of West Virginia University. He is the author (with Brandon Sample, Esq.) of *Pardons and Commutations of Sentences: The Complete Guidebook to Applying for Clemency*, which Amazon named the #1 New Release in Criminal Law. Mr. Mathis has spent more than 25 years assisting federal and state inmates in their fight for freedom.

www.ingramcontent.com/pod-product-compliance
Lightning Source LLC
Chambersburg PA
CBHW080624030426
42336CB00018B/3066